"A VALUABLE HISTORICAL WORK ... A FAS-CINATING ACCOUNT ... Its sensitive treatment of the people who journeyed here makes their dreams and their spirit come alive again."

—John V. Lindsay

Strangers at the Door

A splendid portrait of America's immigrant heritage ... the dream, the reality, the hardships and successes of our nation's greatest strength—human beings in search of freedom and opportunity.

STRANGERS

Ellis Island, Castle Garden, and the

by Ann Novotny

AT THE DOOR

Great Migration to America—

(ABRIDGED EDITION)

Bantam Pathfinder Editions
Toronto / New York / London

RLI:
$$\frac{\text{VLM 11 (VLR 9-11)}}{\text{IL 9-adult}}$$

STRANGERS AT THE DOOR
*A Bantam Book / published by arrangement with
The Chatham Press, Inc.*

PRINTING HISTORY
Chatham Press edition published January 1972
History Book Club edition published May 1972
Abridged Bantam edition published March 1974

Published simultaneously in the United States and Canada

*Bantam Books are published by Bantam Books, Inc. Its trade-
mark, consisting of the words "Bantam Books" and the por-
trayal of a bantam, is registered in the United States Patent
Office and in other countries. Marca Registrada. Bantam
Books, Inc., 666 Fifth Avenue, New York, New York 10019.*

PRINTED IN THE UNITED STATES OF AMERICA

CONTENTS

Compagnie Générale Transatlantique

French Line

Paris — Le Havre — New-York

I
Ellis Island
at Its Busiest
[1907]

They had been at sea for more than two weeks, so long that the passing days had become hard to remember. The old steamship never stopped rolling, and on the roughest days wind and chilling rain kept all the immigrants below deck. Down here in steerage every pitching motion of the ship felt ten times worse. The exhausted passengers lying in narrow bunks near the bow were thankful that their berths were no wider: being so tightly wedged in, shoulder-to-shoulder with their neighbors, prevented them from being tossed out onto the floor. With the tiny portholes closed against bad weather, the foul air was more stifling than ever. Although the steerage area had been whitewashed and its floors scrubbed in port, it was a filthy place now, reeking of old food, seasickness and unwashed humanity. Many of the women had not left their bunks for several days, unable to face

An idealized poster advertising an immigrant
ship, published in Switzerland soon after 1900.
In actuality, the steerage deck was usually
too small for dancing, and what music the
immigrants heard was likely to be played on their
own tin whistles and fiddles.

*(Courtesy of Compagnie
Générale Transatlantique, Paris)*

meals of lukewarm soup, boiled potatoes, herring or lumps of stringy beef, served with thick slices of black bread. One old Hungarian soldier sustained himself on nothing but his own bottle of sweet brandy and a string of vile-looking sausages in his knapsack. Children wailed incessantly in the "married quarters"; their parents looked haggard from the lack of fresh air and sleep. Only a few of the strongest young men, still jubilant over their escape from Czarist Russia, gathered in a small group on deck in the evening to talk once more about their future and sing the old revolutionary songs: "We have shaken the shackles off our feet, we are entering upon a new world, a free world, where man is free!" A sea gull had followed the ship that day . . . the journey was almost over.

Unable to sleep, a young Russian lay in his bunk remembering many things that had happened in the past few months. He had been saving every possible ruble for over two years, knowing that one day he would sail for America. Then a letter had come from his cousin Dimitri in Philadelphia telling of good jobs and free evening classes for mechanics, and enclosing a small creased photograph of Dimitri in a new suit. The young Russian had made up his mind that day, and had gone to the police station for permission to leave his country. After months of waiting and arguing, he had bribed the right offical and at last his exit papers were in his hand. For some of his shipmates, however, leaving home had been more difficult. One, evading conscription into the imperial army, leaped into a cold river at night and swam across to German soil. Another, whose exit papers were refused because his high school education made him too valuable to release, walked to a small border village and bribed the Polish soldiers to look the other way while he crossed.

The sleepless young man relived the long days and nights on the emigrant train to Hamburg. He remembered the men sitting shoulder-to-shoulder on wooden benches along each wall of the cramped, jolting railway car, smoking pipes and talking as the train slowly took them westward to the sea. They ate their small supplies of hard bread and cheese, and fought thirst when their water bottles were empty. The married men wondered how their wives and children were managing in the other cars. At night, they slept as well as they could, wedged onto a section of narrow bench or curled up on their baggage on the floor. The spring nights were cold, but no heat came from the old iron stove in the center of the car. One day their train was shunted onto a siding in a village for hours, but the doors remained locked and they could not get out to stretch in the sunshine where German children stood gaping at the cars marked *Russische Auswanderer* under every window. Now and then came a sudden jolt, as the train hitched up extra cars of emigrants —Austrians, Ukrainians, Hungarians and Bohemians, all now several days away from homes they would never see again. Those who came from small villages had never even seen a train before. When they finally reached the outskirts of Hamburg, the villagers pushed for space at the train's small high windows to stare in awe at the city's great buildings and crowded streets.

The young man smiled to himself as he remembered their arrival at the Hamburg-American shipping line's *Auswanderer-Hallen* in the suburbs of Veddel—a modern "village" where four thousand emigrants at a time were housed, fed, bathed, medically examined and questioned for the official passenger lists, while their baggage and clothing were fumigated. How some of the old peasant women shrieked when they saw their first electric lights, the showers and the steam radiators! There was even a shop selling clothes, and daily band concerts on the lawn outside. The young man knew how much luckier he had been than thousands of other emigrants who were then going by train to ports all over Europe—Bremen, Antwerp, Rotterdam, Le Havre, Liverpool, Glasgow, Southampton, Copenhagen, Constantinople, Piraeus, Fiume and dozens of smaller harbors. In many ports these travelers would sleep in appalling conditions, in wooden barracks or dirty boarding houses, living on little but hard bread, soup and coffee, and waiting as long as three weeks for a ship.

His own ship had been ready to sail from Hamburg the very next day. He remembered his amazement at the ship's great size, as the ferry came down the Elbe River and swung

Emigrants leaving Le Havre around 1900 have their
eyes examined by French Line doctors.
Steamship companies inspected steerage
passengers carefully before departure because they
had to carry home, free of charge, any
immigrants who were rejected at Ellis Island.

*(Courtesy of Compagnie
Générale Transatlantique, Paris)*

under the steamer's stern. Why, it was as long as a village
street and taller than the tallest church, with its huge smoke
funnels sticking up like spires! When the ferry had made
several trips, more than nine hundred men, women and
children with their baggage had scrambled up the steep
gangplank at the ship's side and disappeared into its
steerage quarters.

After they were all below, they listened to the ferry
bumping alongside again, bringing aboard some 350 privileged passengers who traveled in the first and second cabin
classes above. These ladies and gentlemen sailed to America
on the same ship, but they might as well have been in a
different world, for theirs was a place of luxury and
comfort that was out of bounds to most of the travelers on

board. The immigrants knew no more of that wonderful world than what they could imagine from glimpses of the upper decks' comfortable steamer chairs, and the strains of music faintly heard in the evenings. To the cabin-class passengers, the immigrants were a source of entertainment. Leaning over the rail on sunny afternoons, ladies in soft traveling gowns and men in subdued suits pointed to the many-colored aprons and kerchiefs brightening the steerage area below. One lady called her maid to bring nuts, oranges and small coins, and amused herself by tossing them down to the crowded deck below, laughing as excited children and adults scrambled for the favors.

Diversions were few for the immigrants. Even on those sunny days when they all crowded onto their small deck, time passed slowly. One woman read aloud from a pamphlet about the United States, published by a missionary society that helped German Catholics when they arrived. But almost half the adults did not know how to read or write. A man played tunes on a tin whistle hour after hour, while single girls giggled at the attentions of the young men who greatly outnumbered them. Other women sewed, older men smoked pipes and played cards, and children pushed in and out of the crowd in games of their own. Mostly the immigrants talked of the future, remembered the recent past, and stared at the waves until bad weather drove them below. It had been a long, exhausting journey. . . .

Soon after dawn the next day, there was a sudden change in the ship's motion and a different sound from the engine. The harbor pilot from Ambrose Lightship had just come aboard. Early risers up on deck cried out in different languages as they caught sight of a gray strip of land (the Long Island, someone said it was called) emerging on the horizon as the sun burned off the morning mist. One word was the same on all tongues: "America!" Many of those peering at the coast broke into tears. Down in steerage there was frenzied excitement as immigrants jostled around bunks, arranging bundles for the last time, washing hands and faces in basins of cold, salty water, combing unwashed hair or smoothing creases out of the prettiest apron, saved for this occasion—all in an attempt to look their best for

5

A typical immigrant mother has her hands
full—with children, food and baggage. The bulky
pillowcase at left probably held cooking pots
and precious household items.
(Brown Brothers)

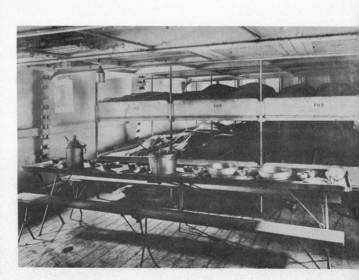

A colorful family of immigrant gypsies from the
kingdom of Serbia (now part of Yugoslavia).
*(Courtesy of National Park Service, Augustus F.
Sherman Collection)*

The stark reality of steerage on the
French Line's La Provence, photographed in 1906.
On some other ships, steerage was below
the water line, with no ventilation. In these bunks,
6 immigrants slept side by side on straw-filled
mattresses under 2 rough blankets.
*(Courtesy of Compagnie Générale
Transatlantique, Paris)*

7

the American inspectors. Money was counted for the hundredth time, then secreted away in some safe inner pocket. The deck became more and more crowded as baggage was carried up and added to the mounting piles of battered suitcases, wicker baskets, cooking pots tied in old blankets and bulky goose-feather pillows bound together with thin rope. Then there was nothing to do for a while except find a place to sit and rehearse once again the best answers to all the questions the inspectors might ask about health, money, work and friends.

By the time the ship entered the Narrows, the harbor entrance between Brooklyn and Staten Island, everyone was up on deck, crowded as closely as possible to the best places by the rail. The view was amazing. They were surrounded on all sides in this mile-wide channel by other ships—some of them so small and old that their names could not be made out, others as large as their own and flying flags of Germany, France, Britain and Sweden. Several of these ships had been anchored all night in the Narrows, waiting for the quarantine clearance that would allow them to sail into the Upper Bay.

It was a morning in the early summer of 1907. The immigrants crowding the decks of all these ships on that day did not know it, but they were entering New York at the peak of the greatest mass movement in human history. One million immigrants had landed in America in 1905, another million in 1906, and by the time 1907 was over another 1,285,349 newcomers would have arrived— 1,004,756 of them disembarking in New York and passing through Ellis Island, the busiest immigrant receiving station in the country. Through Ellis Island's doors poured a steady stream of an average five thousand immigrants daily, seven days a week. Week after week the numbers kept climbing, and on April 17, 1907, the most active day of all, 11,745 newcomers were admitted. The harbor was often choked with ships crammed with as many as twenty thousand passengers waiting to be ferried to Ellis Island; many immigrants had to spend an extra night in steerage because there was no room for them on the Island.

**A young Russian Jewish girl arriving at Ellis Island
in 1905. Photo by Lewis Hine.**
*(New York Public Library, Local History
& Genealogy Division)*

Heads on deck turned as a small cutter came alongside.
A ladder was raised against the ship's rail, and two men and
a woman in uniforms climbed aboard and pushed their way
quickly through the crowd of immigrants toward the
second cabin-class area. A murmur of apprehension ran
through the watching crowd, but the officers barely glanced
at the immigrants. Their business was with cabin-class
passengers only, and the immigrants' turn would come
later, at Ellis Island. In the saloon, the immigration inspector asked two or three brief questions of each waiting
second-cabin passenger, while the other man, a doctor for
the U.S. Public Health Service, looked quickly at their eyes
as they filed past. Full information about these travelers
was listed, as required by law, on the ship's official
passenger list or "manifest." Because the shipping companies had made a great fuss when regular inspections in
this class had begun about five years earlier, the inspector
did his job as quickly as possible. He hardly looked at a
small hunchbacked Polish woman from Danzig, who said
that her husband and children would meet her at the pier;

9

Taken off a ship infected with a contagious disease
Italian immigrants wait on the side-wheeler
James W. Wadsworth at the U.S. Quarantine
Station's dock on Staten Island. Photo by Alice Austen.
(Staten Island Historical Society)

he did not know or care that this woman had been deported from Ellis Island because of her deformity two years earlier, when the whole family had arrived in steerage, and that her husband had finally saved enough money to bring her into the country this easy way. If the woman could afford to travel in style, she would obviously never become a public charge. When the last second-cabin passenger had been passed, the inspector ran his eyes down the first-cabin list of Americans and wealthy foreign visitors who were coming to tour or settle in this country (no one ever called *them* "immigrants"), and simply muttered, "Okay, that'll do." The Public Health Service officer was chatting with the ship's doctor, making sure that there had been no cases of epidemic diseases such as cholera, yellow fever or typhoid. If any serious contagious illnesses had been reported, the patients would have been taken at once on the quarantine boat, the *James W. Wadsworth*, to hospital wards on Hoffman Island, while other passengers would have been held in strict isolation on nearby Swinburn Island until the danger of their developing symptoms had passed. As it was, the doctor said the ship's hospital contained only one second-cabin woman with suspected appendicitis. This patient, in the care of the matron, was led down to the cutter and the small launch headed straight for Ellis Island's hospital.

The liner had been moving slowly north into the Upper Bay while this inspection was taking place. As the enormous harbor came into view, expressions of wonder and awe could be heard on the steerage deck, and people in the center pushed and craned to get a better look at the spectacular sight. Mothers lifted small children into the air to see. There on the left was the towering Statue of Liberty, lifting her torch of freedom to the sky. The bay itself was filled with other steamships, tugs and paddle-wheeled ferries crossing in all directions; an excursion boat passed, carrying a happy crowd to Coney Island. Rising on the skyline five miles away were the office buildings of lower Manhattan, taller than anything in Hamburg; so tall, in fact, that they looked like a ridge of small hills. The highest one of all, the new Singer Building, would reach

Ellis Island, photographed in the early 1900's
by its Chief Clerk, Augustus F. Sherman. New
Jersey's docks are in the background at right.
*(Courtesy of National Park Service, Augustus F.
Sherman Collection)*

An Italian family on the ferry from
the docks to Ellis Island, photographed by
Lewis Hine in 1905.
*(New York Public Library, Local History
& Genealogy Division)*

forty-seven stories when it was finished the next year. Also
on the left of their view, just beyond the Statue of Liberty,
were the red brick buildings of Ellis Island where the
immigrants would be taken. They had all heard of the
Island and knew its name. That was the famous Island of
Tears—*Tränen Insel* to the Germans, *Isola delle Lagrime* to
the Italians—where those whom the inspectors judged too
weak, old or poor to support themselves would be detained,

then deported back to Europe to rebuild a broken life there.

Before the immigrants were taken to Ellis Island, all the cabin-class passengers disembarked in the city. Swinging into the Hudson River, the liner docked at one of a row of piers and the immigrants were pushed back from the rail (for fear they might leap onto the dock, someone said), while the privileged travelers went down the gangway and vanished into the sheds. Then it was the immigrants' turn: guards shouted in many languages, "Hurry up there! Move along, stupid! Don't dawdle!" as they pushed them along into a roped enclosure at the end of the dock. A former shepherd in the jostling crowd was reminded of the way he used to herd his sheep into the farmyard back home. The crowd stood there patiently in the warm sun, wondering how long the waiting would last. Most of the immigrants carried all their luggage with them, but some had large old trunks and wooden boxes which were now swung out of the ship's hold and dumped onto the dock beside them. A customs officer stared at them without interest. Some minutes later the baggage was loaded onto the lower deck of a small ferryboat, and as many of the immigrants as possible were hustled, with more shouting and pushing, onto the upper deck. When the boat was full, the rest of them were loaded onto two barges waiting behind. Wedged together at the rail, they began the ride down the river. For one hour on the pier they had been standing on American soil: now at Ellis Island they would be told whether they could stay for life.

> Overleaf: The Registry Hall, holding 5,000 people, was the biggest room most immigrants had ever seen—200 feet long, 100 feet wide, with a 56-foot-high vaulted ceiling. In 1911, the central stairway was moved under the gallery, doubling the usable floor space, while the iron rails were replaced by wooden benches shown in this photograph. Off the gallery were dormitories for those detained.
>
> *(Courtesy of National Park Service, Augustus F. Sherman Collection)*

As they approached Ellis Island, the ferryboat slowed to a standstill. The side of the dock was so crowded with other boats and barges that there was no more room to tie up. The boat rocked in place from the gentle swell of passing ships, the sun became hotter, and some of the children began to wail more shrilly. There was no place to sit down—no room even to move—no toilet in sight, no water, and they had had nothing to eat since breakfast. When they finally landed, the ground still seemed to sway under their feet as they dragged children and bundles along the walk toward the imposing red brick building. There was more shouting and pushing from guards who made them stand together in groups according to big numbers on the tags tied to their coats. An interpreter yelled out the numbers in German, Polish, Hungarian, Italian and Russian. During all this commotion an elderly Rumanian, wearing a heavy sheepskin coat in spite of the heat, dropped his bundle with a metallic crash and fell to the ground beside it. There was a little eddy of excitement around him, until two uniformed men carried the elderly man away toward the connecting island on the ferry slip's far side, where the hospital buildings stood. Then the shouting began once more and, one by one, groups of thirty people at a time moved slowly forward, through the big door into dark tiled corridors, then—jostling two or three abreast—up a steep flight of stairs.

Their eyes blinking in the sudden bright light, they paused for a moment at the top. Sunshine streamed through the arched windows of the largest room they had ever seen. An unbelievable crowd of men, women and children was on all sides—enough to populate ten villages back home—and the hall was so huge that it might have contained their farm animals as well. Their old town square on market days, even the bustling streets of the port, had been nothing like this. There were Hungarians in high boots and rough jackets, Russians in fur caps, Greeks in short white kilts and slippers with pompons on them, Cossack soldiers with fierce mustaches and swords, one old Serb with a rifle, gypsy families and women everywhere in brightly colored babushkas. Everyone was talking at once.

A few people were crying. The whole place was humming like a giant beehive, and over the occasional baby's wail names of people from all corners of the Old World were shouted: "Antek Milkowski!" "Srulovitz!" "Konstantin Lafkas!" "Berges!" "Policano!" "Pakalns!" Leaning over a balcony rail above all this commotion were a few well-dressed Americans, watching the ever-changing scene with curiosity and amusement.

The immigrants at the top of the stairs were not given any more time to stand and stare. "This way! Hurry up!" an interpreter shouted in several languages, and they were pushed along one of the dozens of metal railings which divided the whole floor into a maze of open passageways. Although they did not realize it, they were already passing their first test as they hastened down the row in single file. Twenty-five feet away a doctor, in the smart blue uniform of the U.S. Public Health Service, was watching them carefully as they approached him. All children who looked over two years old were taken from their mothers' arms and made to walk.

It took only a few moments for the immigrants to reach the doctor, but that was time enough for his sharp eyes to notice one man who was breathing too heavily, a woman who was trying to hide her limp behind a big bundle, and a young girl whose shuffle and bewildered gaze might have been symptoms of a feeble mind. As each immigrant paused in front of him, the doctor looked hard at his face, hair, neck and hands; at the same time, with an interpreter at his side to help, he asked short questions about the immigrant's age or work to test his alertness. When a mother came up with children, each child in turn, starting with the oldest, was asked his name to make sure that he was not deaf or dumb.

In the doctor's hand was a piece of chalk; on the coats of about two out of every ten or eleven immigrants who passed him he scrawled a large white letter—"H" for possible heart trouble, "L" for lameness, a circled "X" for suspected mental defects, or "F" for a bad rash on the face. Then the immigrants filed on to a second doctor who was looking for diseases specifically mentioned in the law as

In October, 1907, these Jewish men were
detained for more detailed medical check-ups.
Under the eye chart with Hebrew lettering
stands an immigrant with "K" chalked on his
jacket, the symbol for suspected hernia.
*(Library of Congress,
Prints & Photographs Division)*

A Hungarian mother and her daughters.
Sometimes entire villages in the Austro-Hungarian
empire emigrated together, for as industry
expanded, the old economy of
the region broke down and many once-prosperous
peasants lost their land and work.
*(Courtesy of National Park Service,
Augustus F. Sherman Collection)*

reasons for deportation: signs of tuberculosis, leprosy, or a
contagious skin disease of the scalp called *favus*.

Again the line moved on; those immigrants who had not
been through medical inspections at European ports trem-
bled as they saw two more doctors waiting in front of a
window, with basins of disinfectant and towels at their
sides. These were the dreaded "eye men" described in so
many terrible rumors, and what they did, some people said,
hurt badly. But it was all over in a few seconds, as those
who had been through the same process in Hamburg or Le

A "primary line" inspector (lower left)
in the Registry Hall questions the young man
whose name is listed on the 22nd line
of the manifest sheet on his desk. An interpreter
(with badge in his jacket lapel) sits next to the
immigrant, ready to help.
(Culver Pictures)

23

Havre had known it would be. The doctors peered, tilted the immigrants' heads back slightly, and swiftly snapped back the upper eyelids over a small instrument (actually a hook for buttoning old-fashioned gloves). Blinking slightly, the immigrants passed on . . . that hadn't been so bad after all. The doctors had been looking at the linings of the eyelids for symptoms of a blinding disease called *trachoma*, very common in those days before a cure was discovered. Immigrants who had it were sure to be sent back to Europe, and whenever the doctors were suspicious they chalked an "E" (for eyes) on the immigrants' coat fronts.

At the end of the aisle interpreters waved immigrants whose coats were unmarked back toward the main part of the Registry Hall. But those whose coats bore chalk letters were pushed aside into a "pen," an area enclosed by a wire screen, to wait for more detailed medical examinations by other doctors. If they had any of the diseases proscribed by the immigration laws, or seemed too ill or feeble-minded to earn their living, they would be deported. One sobbing mother was pushed into the enclosure to wait with her little girl of eight or nine. The law said a parent had to accompany any very young child who was deported; but children of ten or older were sent back to Europe alone and simply released in the port from which they had sailed. Several weeping families in the hall were trying to make a terrible decision—"Shall we all go back together? Who will stay?"

Those immigrants waiting on benches for their final test talked anxiously and rehearsed for the last time their answers to probable questions about jobs, cash and relatives. Some said it was best to answer questions as fully as possible. Others said that inspectors were just like lawyers, always trying to trip you up, and it was best to keep your mouth shut and just say "Yes" and "No" so they couldn't muddle you. Could American officials be bribed with a gold coin or two? You had to be very, very careful. You had to show some money, but perhaps it wasn't safe to show it at all. The waiting time, often an hour or two on busy days like these, seemed endless to the nervous immigrants; many of them leaned against their bundles in exhaustion and tried

This Italian mother, as the photographer recorded, had trouble finding her luggage among the huge stacks that covered most of the main building's ground floor. Luggage was forwarded from here to any railroad station in America. Photo by Lewis Hine, 1905.

(New York Public Library, Local History & Genealogy Division)

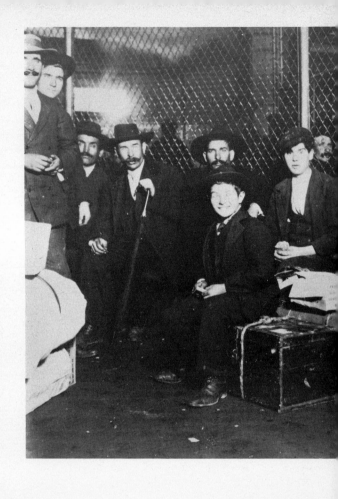

Italians in the railroad Waiting Room open box
lunches they have just bought for the last
stage of their journey. Immigrants who preferred
to buy single items of food could choose
apples at 2¢ apiece, kosher bologna at
13¢ per pound, sandwiches and pies of any
kind for 4¢ each. The Waiting Room was
divided into areas for each of the
railroads, which ferried passengers to their
terminals in Hoboken and
Jersey City. Photo by Lewis Hine, 1905.
*(New York Public Library, Local History &
Genealogy Division)*

to sleep.

At last an interpreter moved them into the adjoining row. He made sure that they all had the same big number pinned on their coats. At the end of the aisle sat an inspector, on whose desk lay the manifest headed by that number. This large sheet of paper had been prepared by the shipping company and contained answers to questions about each of the thirty immigrants listed on it. As the first immigrant from the group approached the high desk, the inspector peered at the tag on his coat, noted the smaller "1" in its bottom corner, put his finger against that man's name on the first line of the form, and wearily prepared to start the questioning again.

The inspector felt harassed and very tired. He had been working from nine in the morning until after seven at night, seven days a week, for so long that he had almost forgotten what he did on his last day off, Easter Sunday. His starched collar was wilting under his heavy serge jacket in the summer heat. To the waiting immigrant he looked hot, cross and stern. The interpreter beside him, who had been working twelve-hour days, looked exhausted too, and his morning had gotten off to a particularly bad start. Coming over to work on the 8:40 ferry from the Barge Office, he had been cornered by two almost hysterical Italians, who recognized him as their countryman and begged him to get their wives released from detention. He told them to find the man from the Society for the Protection of Italian Immigrants, whose desk was on the ground floor, but they clung to his sleeve, pleading with him to do them a special favor, until he had to push them away as the ferry docked. There wasn't enough time in the day for him to do even his own job properly, he had grumbled, as he described the incident to another Italian interpreter, young Fiorello La Guardia. Before this long day was over, the interpreter would have helped the inspector question between four and five hundred immigrants, so that between them the two officials had only about two minutes in which to decide whether each immigrant was "clearly and beyond a doubt entitled to land," as the law specified. Every doubtful case was detained for further questioning.

The rapid queries, designed to verify the most important of the twenty-nine bits of information about each immigrant on the manifest, began: "What work do you do?" "Do you have a job waiting for you?" "Who paid for your passage here?" "Is anyone meeting you?" "Where are you going?" "Can you read and write?" "Have you ever been in prison?" "How much money do you have?" "Show it to me now." "Where did you get it?"

Nearly all of the immigrants quickly got curt nods from the inspector, who handed them landing cards, and sudden friendly smiles from the interpreter. They were in! "Praise God," murmured an elderly Ruthenian farmer, bending suddenly over the desk and kissing the back of the inspector's hand in gratitude. For most of the group, the ordeal was over. After only three or four hours on Ellis Island, they were free to go.

The first stop on the way out was the Money Exchange at one end of the hall, marked with a big sign that no one could miss, no matter what language he read: *Cambia Valuta – Wechelgeschäft – Bureau de Change – Penningar Vexlas–Penz Valto Uzlet–Lamiana Pienendzy*. Gold, silver and paper money from all over Europe was exchanged there for American dollars by six cashiers, who chalked up that day's official rates on a blackboard. A small Post Office counter was nearby, and a few immigrants took a moment to scribble notes and send the good news home at once. Downstairs, immigrants with extra trunks went to the baggage room to claim and make arrangements for them to

Overleaf: "Seven soldiers lost to the Kaiser," the German Consul in New York is said to have sighed, when he saw this photograph. Jakob Mithelstadt and his family, Russian Germans, landed from the Pretoria on May 9, 1905, and were admitted to go to Kuln, North Dakota. Since 1820, almost 7 million immigrants have come to the U.S. from Germany; their peak decade was the 1880's.
(Courtesy of National Park Service, Augustus F. Sherman Collection)

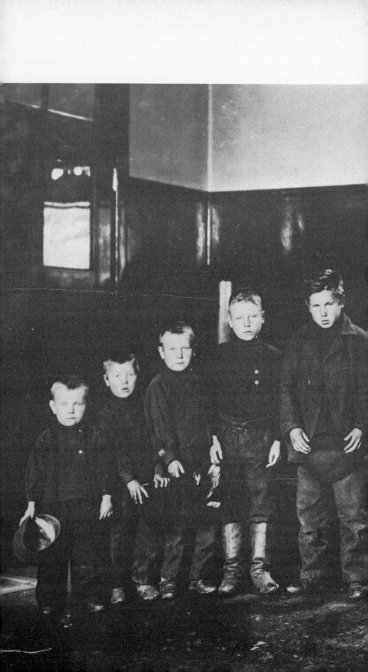

be sent on to their destinations. Two out of every three immigrants were traveling beyond New York City, and railroad tickets to places all across the country were sold by a dozen agents in the Railroad Room. On the busiest days, the agents figured, they sold twenty-five tickets a minute among them. Sometimes the pace slowed, though, while they scratched their heads and tried to discover where an immigrant really wanted to go. One Italian insisted that his destination was "Pringvilliamas"—that was Springfield, Mass. A Hungarian woman clutched a slip of paper reading "Szekenevno Pillsburs," which took a long time to decipher as Second Avenue, Pittsburgh. Experience helped the ticket agents make intelligent guesses. They knew, for example, that rosy-cheeked Germans with large families were almost invariably going to farms in the northwest, and that helped them translate such names as "Linkinbra" to Lincoln, Nebraska. But once in a while they made a mistake: fifteen Italian immigrants who wanted to go to Amsterdam Avenue, New York City, found themselves in Amsterdam in upstate New York.

With their tickets and big, cheap box lunches in hand, immigrants sat in the large Waiting Room in areas marked for each independent railroad line. When the time for their train's departure was reasonably near, they would be ferried on barges to the terminal stations in Jersey City or Hoboken, from there to go on the last stage of their journeys to the west or south. Immigrants going to New England went on the ferry to Manhattan.

Those who were going to stay in New York City were in some ways the luckiest. They walked down the dark corridor and through doors marked "Push, To New York"—there, pressed against the far side of the wire screen separating them from the walk to the ferry, were dozens of waiting friends and relatives who had obtained passes to come to the Island. They met with tears and hugs and shrieks of recognition, and the half-hour ride on the ferry to lower Manhattan was always a time of supreme happiness. They pushed each other in a race to be the first off at the Barge Office landing slip. Waiting in Battery Park was another crowd of welcomers; shouts went up for a brother or cousin who hadn't been seen for fifteen years, and there was a general bedlam of cries. Tears of joy and relief flowed down almost every face. More commotion came from the area where top-heavy piles of baggage were loaded onto horse-drawn wagons, and when the elevated train rumbled overhead there were loud gasps of amazement. Some of the newcomers found themselves pulled by their arms into the nearest washroom or quiet corner of the park, where friends tugged off their old black caps or peasant skirts, insisting that these be changed on the spot for more acceptable "American" garments. They didn't want to be the laughingstock of the neighborhood, did they? Half an hour after the ferry *Ellis Island* had unloaded a fresh crowd of immigrants, the public dressing rooms and even the sidewalks around the park were littered with abandoned kerchiefs, visored caps and occasional shirts and trousers. So the citizens-to-be set off into the New World, marveling at the tall buildings, the clean-shaven men, the first small black child, or an amazing automobile, while their friends joked about their astonishment. There would be food, talk, laughter and important questions about jobs, as late into the night more and more friends came to welcome the strangers. Then, at last, would come much-needed baths and sleep in beds that no longer rolled with the waves. Tomorrow, life in America would begin.

But the beginning was delayed, perhaps forever, for the unfortunate immigrants who were kept behind at Ellis Island. As one manifest group passed, for example, the inspector singled out a pretty Swedish girl who said she was going to Chicago alone to get married; he ordered her detained until her fiancé or a representative from the Lutheran Pilgrim House came to get her. Immigration officials refused to send single women alone into the streets of strange cities. If the Swedish girl's boy friend came east to meet her, an interpreter would probably escort the young couple to City Hall to be married on the spot to prevent any deception (in earlier days hundreds of marriages were performed on Ellis Island itself to combat "white slavery"). A second detained immigrant was an old Russian Jew whose threadbare pockets contained only

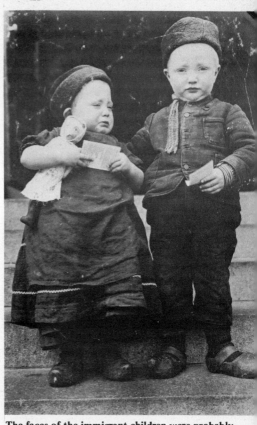

The faces of the immigrant children were probably
the most expressive. Clutching her doll
and a religious leaflet, a little Dutch girl tries not
to cry, while comforted by her brother.
*(Courtesy of National Park Service, Augustus F.
Sherman Collection)*

A Russian Jew at Ellis Island in 1905,
photographed by Lewis Hine.
*(New York Public Library, Local History
& Genealogy Division)*

seventy-five cents. His American relatives in Rhode Island would send him money for a train ticket, he said. Terrified that the inspector was not going to admit him, he began to sob out the story of his family's murder in the 1905 *pogrom*, wailing that the Americans might as well kill him then and there as send him back. A man from the Hebrew Immigrant Aid Society came running up at the sound of the commotion. He soothed the old man, saying that he would send a telegram at once to his relatives, and that the old man would be well looked after on the Island until the

A Board of Special Inquiry—consisting of 3 inspectors, a stenographer and interpreter— hears the case of the detained immigrant girl in the foreground. Over 70,000 cases were heard in a busy year like 1907.
(Brown Brothers)

money arrived. A few minutes later, a nervous young Italian, sweating with excitement, answered pressing questions about the work he could do by waving a well-thumbed letter under the inspector's nose. An Italian uncle in Pittsfield—"See, right here"—had promised him a job on a construction gang. A frown passed over the inspector's face as he ordered the young man detained for the Board of Special Inquiry. "But why? Why?" the young man shouted. As the interpreter said that the Contract Labor Law would be explained at the hearing, the young man's heart sank. He had forgotten! He had been warned to lie about this! Immigrants had to show that they were strong and clever enough to find work easily, but it was against the law for them to have agreed before they left home to take a specific job in exchange for their passage. This law had been in effect for over twenty years. It was meant to protect immigrants from slavelike labor, and to protect American workers from gangs of European laborers imported by a "boss" to break strikes or keep wages low. If this young man had sailed with several friends, all of whom were bound for Pittsfield, the inspector would have felt sure that the *padrone* system was at work, and the whole group would probably have been sent back to Italy together.

The Swedish girl, the old Russian and the unlucky Italian were typical of those immigrants (about two out of every ten) who were held at the Island for more than a few hours. More than half of them, like the girl and the old man, were detained for two or three days for their own protection. The others, such as the young Italian, who faced more questioning before a Board of Special Inquiry, rarely numbered more than one out of every ten people admitted. Immigrants were brought before the board for many different reasons, including violations of the Contract Labor Law. A telegram from Europe might have brought word that an immigrant was a criminal wanted by the police in his own country; perhaps a man's wife had reported that he was deserting her. Sometimes inspectors felt that an immigrant was really a pauper who had been given a steamship ticket and a suit of clothes by a foreign government eager to get him off its charity rolls. Unfortu-

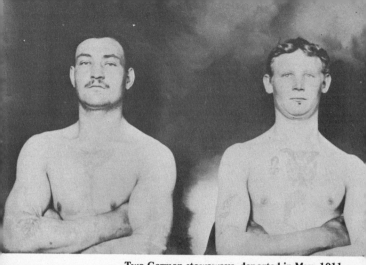

Two German stowaways, deported in May, 1911.
While stowaways were legally entitled to enter
the U.S. if they could pass the inspection,
Commissioner Williams ordered most of
them deported as likely to become public charges.
(Courtesy of National Park Service, Augustus F.
Sherman Collection)

nate people physically or mentally handicapped in earning a
living would be deported if they seemed "likely to become
public charges." The law ordered deportation for anyone
who was a criminal, a prostitute, or suffering from insanity
or a contagious disease. A few immigrants were sent back
because of their political or religious beliefs: they were
usually anarchists who wanted to overthrow organized
government, or polygamists who believed that a man should
have several wives.

A detained immigrant went into a small side office to
face the Board of Special Inquiry, made up of three
inspectors and an interpreter sitting behind a long desk. He
swore on the Bible or a crucifix to tell the truth, then
answered questions about his right to land, as a stenographer recorded his words. No lawyers were present, but an
immigrant's friends and relatives were often brought to the

Island to testify in his behalf. The votes of two out of three inspectors decided a case, but if the third inspector or the immigrant himself felt that a sentence of deportation was unfair, he could appeal the decision to the Secretary of Commerce and Labor in Washington. At this stage, the immigrant was allowed to hire a lawyer to help him. In fact, the Secretary often sustained an immigrant's appeal, or ordered a new hearing to be held if fresh evidence was presented. Sometimes the immigrant would be admitted after a bond was posted guaranteeing that he would not become dependent on public charity. Inspectors who were chosen by Ellis Island's commissioner to serve on the Boards of Special Inquiry, like their colleagues in the Registry Hall, worked under great pressure in these busy years and had to rely mainly on their common sense. In a single year, seventy thousand or more cases would be heard. The system was not too cruel: about five out of every six immigrants whose cases were heard were admitted by the boards after careful questioning. The greatest number of exclusions happened in 1911, when about thirteen thousand immigrants (just over 2 per cent of the 650,000 who arrived that year) were sent back to their homelands.

The fact that they were a small minority did not comfort those who were deported and whose stories of hardship were often pathetically reported in the newspapers. Americans might have agreed that laws were needed to exclude "undesirables," but all hearts bled when a family was torn apart and, for example, an eleven-year-old daughter who was slightly retarded was dispatched back to Poland alone. Immigrant-aid or missionary societies, often founded to protect the interests of a particular ethnic group, raised bitter protests when one of their people was deported, while the foreign-language press stirred up public sympathy over every case of hardship. Ellis Island's inspectors, kindhearted as many of them were, had the unenviable job of enforcing laws that grew stricter as the years passed. The unlucky immigrants they had to deport were detained on Ellis Island, often for two or three weeks, until they could be sent back to Europe on a ship of the line that had brought them. The shipping companies, who were supposed to screen out all "undesirables" in Europe, had to transport the immigrants home without charge and to pay for the cost of keeping them on the Island until their next ships arrived.

The job of housing and feeding all the detained immigrants was almost too much for the officials at Ellis Island. There wasn't enough room even for the immigrants who passed through without delay. The architects who designed the buildings in 1897 had planned them to accommodate no more than 500,000 foreigners in one year—they had believed that the flood tide of immigration was over. No one guessed that the high point of the greatest mass movement in history was just about to begin. For inspectors and immigrants alike, it was a nightmare: the sound of hammering hardly ever stopped on the Island, as alterations and new construction went on as quickly as possible. For a while in 1904, rooms were so overcrowded during the day that detained immigrants were moved out to the sidewalk for a few hours.

Commissioner Robert Watchorn, who took over the running of Ellis Island in 1905, described his task as "stupendous"—there was not enough room, time or money, and the bureaucrats above him could hardly believe his reports. At the end of 1906, he seriously considered hiring barges to serve as extra detention quarters, until an appropriation of $400,000 let him start construction of a new Baggage and Dormitory Building. By the spring of 1907, as the greatest flood of immigrants started arriving, Watchorn was almost distraught. That year 195,540 people were detained. He was using "every available bit of space at the entire station," Watchorn told his superiors, and he begged Washington for more money for a larger refrigeration plant (barely one day's supply of food could be kept on the Island), a larger hospital, more toilets and a second ferryboat.

The commissioner tried to shock his superiors into supplying funds by reporting that respectable women and impressionable teenage girls were being detained in the same dormitories as hardened prostitutes sentenced to deportation. Temporary one-story wooden barracks had been hastily erected in 1903 beside the main building, providing another seven hundred bunks for those detained overnight. There was then sleeping space for eighteen hundred immigrants, squeezed into three-tiered bunks only two feet apart, and even these beds were not enough, so that many unlucky immigrants were forced to sleep on benches, tables or the floor. It was worse than steerage. On one unforgettable night, seventeen hundred women and

The Dining Hall, photographed in February, 1907. Dinner at 11:30 a.m. consisted of thick soups and stews, although in earlier years profit-minded concessionaires had served little but stewed prunes with bread. While all immigrants would eat kosher beef, Scandinavians preferred dried fish, Chinese asked for rice, Italians grumbled at the lack of wine, and one group of Mohammedan dervishes, forbidden to eat food over which the shadow of an infidel had passed, lived on boiled eggs.

(Library of Congress, Prints & Photographs Division)

In spite of the fact that black American citizens
had fewer rights than the newest white
immigrant, a steady trickle of black immigrants
arrived at Castle Garden and Ellis Island.
These women, photographed at Ellis Island
on April 6, 1911, came on the steamship Korona

children slept in a dormitory with bunks for six hundred.
The crowding was producing "an intolerable situation,"
Watchorn concluded, "a condition which no private corporation would have permitted to continue for a single day
if the laws relating to health and decent comfort in any city
of the United States had been applied to it."

A financial panic eased the pressure somewhat while
Washington was still wondering what to do. Letters from
newly arrived immigrants reached Europe quickly and, just
as tales of all the good jobs available in America's expand-
ing industries had caused the great rise in immigration for
the previous three years, now news of the economic
"crash" caused a sudden drop in the arrivals for 1908. But
this depression did not last long, and the yearly statistics on
immigrants soon started rising again—more than 600,000
passed through Ellis Island in 1911 and again in 1912, and

from Guadeloupe, French West Indies.
Famous black immigrants of this period include
nationalist leader Marcus Garvey and the poet
Claude McKay, both from Jamaica.
*(Courtesy of National Park Service, Augustus F.
Sherman Collection)*

by 1914 the number was well over 800,000. But it never
again rose over a million a year, and Ellis Island was now
better equipped to receive those who did arrive. In 1911 a
third floor was added to the northwest wing of the main
building, creating much more room for the Boards of
Special Inquiry. Downstairs there was space for an Information Office, for anxious relatives and friends. When the
medical offices were moved down to larger quarters on the
ground floor, the entire Registry Hall was left free for
inspectors questioning immigrants. Money was granted for a
third story to be added to the Dormitory and Baggage
Building in 1914, and in the same year a third story was
under construction on the southeast wing of the main
building. There was now more room than ever before—and
suddenly the immigrants stopped coming. The Great War
was under way in Europe.

II
The Earliest Immigrants
[to 1855]

The story of immigration to America begins long before the era of Ellis Island. The earliest immigrants had been here for several hundred centuries when the first Europeans beached their ships on the east coast of what they called the "New World." Perhaps as long ago as fifty thousand years before the birth of Christ (and certainly by 20,000 B.C.), the ancestors of American Indians began migrating to the then empty continent. They came for essentially the same reasons as later immigrants—fleeing their enemies or seeking richer hunting grounds. But they came by land, walking across the great causeway of rock or solid ice that once linked the northeast corner of Siberia to Alaska. Small

On Christopher Columbus's third voyage
to the Caribbean in 1498, he found Indians
diving for oysters off Isla Margarita.
The Spaniards, exploring to find treasure, traded
weapons for beautiful pearl necklaces they saw
the Indian women wearing. This engraving by
Theodore De Bry is from the German edition of
Historia de Indias by Bartolomé de las Casas,
a Dominican monk who preserved
the only existing version of Columbus's diary.
(Library of Congress, Rare Book Division)

Leif Ericsson in 1000 A.D. became the first
European to discover North America—by mistake.
The earliest immigrants followed a few
years later, but they were defeated by Indians and
harsh weather. The Vikings, or Norsemen,
were then the best sailors and shipbuilders
in the world: this typical boat, doubling as a tent on
an American beach, was drawn by a 19th-century artist.
*(Library of Congress,
Prints & Photographs Division)*

groups of these Asian wanderers continued crossing for
many centuries, until their natural bridge to America was
washed away into the fifty-mile-wide Bering Strait. Struggling against a harsh climate and predatory animals, they
settled the western hemisphere down to Tierra del Fuego,
and their culture reached great heights in the Mayan, Aztec
and Incan civilizations. These empires, and most of the
population, were located in Central and South America,
but—by the time the first Europeans landed—about one

million Indians were living in the territories that later became the United States and southern Canada.

In the summer of the year 1000, an ancient saga relates, a small group of Viking ships beached somewhere on the continent's northeastern coast. The captain of this expedition, Leif Ericsson, had set sail from Norway to carry news of the Christian faith to his former home in Greenland, but he was blown off his course and landed on a strange shore—possibly Nova Scotia or Cape Cod. He called the new place Vinland or Wineland, for the wild grapes his hungry men found growing near the beach. Leif Ericsson left America as soon as his crew was refreshed, and so did another legendary explorer of that coast, Biarni Heriulfson. But the first immigrants who intended to found a permanent colony arrived a few years later—160 Greenlanders in three ships, led by a trader called Thorfinn Karlsefni. Unfortunately, they landed on an inhospitable, rocky shore (possibly Labrador), and when they sailed south, seeking the land of grapes, they were attacked by ferocious Indian warriors. After three years of Indian attacks and miserable living conditions, Karlsefni's group abandoned its settlement and returned home.

Five hundred years later, three Spanish caravels anchored off a small island in the Bahamas on October 12, 1492. They had been at sea for ten weeks, and their captain, Christopher Columbus, believed that by sailing westward around the unknown half of the world he had reached the Orient. It may have been prophetic of the "nation of nations" one day to be built to the north that this Italian-born admiral, sailing under a Spanish flag, had an Irishman, an Englishman, a Jew and a Negro in his crew. Ninety sailors in all manned the *Santa María*, *Niña* and *Pinta* that year. On a second, much larger expedition in 1493, Columbus left a few of his men to establish a colony on Hispaniola (the island of Haiti) where they earned a bad name for themselves by enslaving the native Indians and forcing them to dig for gold. These colonists, and others who soon joined them, were not true immigrants: their purpose in exploring for the east coast of "the Indies" had been to find a shortcut to its legendary treasures of gold,

The earliest drawings by an eyewitness of North
American Indians were made in 1564 by a
French artist, Jacques Le Moyne de Morgues. He
showed Indians in Florida worshiping
a column erected by the French 2 years

earlier. The few French settlers in Florida,
austere Huguenots, were slaughtered in 1565
by Spanish soldiers who founded Saint
Augustine, the oldest city in the United States.

*(Library of Congress,
Prints & Photographs Division)*

silver, pearls, silks and spices, and they intended to stay only long enough to make themselves rich. The fabled court of the Great Khan was nowhere to be found. But when Cortés conquered the Aztec empire of Mexico and Pizarro subdued the Peruvian Incas, glittering piles of gold and silver were shipped back to Spain. Many of the colonists on Hispaniola abandoned their diggings and rushed to open up mines in the richer territories of the South American mainland.

The heavily laden ships of the Spanish settlers carried back to Europe ten times as much precious metal as was then being mined in all the rest of the world. But vessels sailing to the New World brought imports that were even more valuable (although no one then realized it) than gold and silver. The Spaniards sent home for wheat seeds, oranges, limes, grapes and olives for their new plantations; they had pigs, mules, longhorn cattle and horses shipped over (some of the horses ran wild and wandered north to the Great Plains, where Indians found and tamed them). More important still, the colonists brought from Spain their religion, forms of government, social customs and skills. As time passed, many of the Spanish men (who outnumbered their own women by at least ten to one) married local Indian women, and a sizable mixed population grew up in the colonies. Although the population grew, there were still not enough men to work the plantations on the islands and coastal areas, and black slaves began to be imported from Africa by the Portuguese in small numbers as early as 1502. The great majority of Spanish immigrants stayed in South and Central America, but their empire gradually extended northward into lands that later became part of the United States. Balboa, Ponce de Leon, De Soto and Coronado led long exploratory marches between 1513 and 1542, and soon Spaniards had sailed up the coasts of North America as far as Oregon and Labrador. Their soldiers guarded the frontiers of New Spain from a chain of remote military outposts such as the one at St. Augustine, Florida (built in 1565), and by 1776, the Franciscan brothers had built missions as far north as Arizona and San Francisco.

The Spanish did not have the New World to themselves,

however. Explorers and adventurers from all the seafaring nations of Europe were quick to follow the route discovered by Columbus. Small numbers of Portuguese settlers colonized Brazil after Pedro Alvares Cabral landed there in 1500. Amerigo Vespucci, a Florentine merchant and navigator, was aboard one Portuguese ship which crossed the South Atlantic in 1501; he wrote letters home describing the continent (occasionally inventing what he had not seen), and his name, "America," stuck to the new hemisphere almost by chance. From France came Italian-born Giovanni da Verrazano, discoverer of New York harbor in 1524, and Jacques Cartier, who found the St. Lawrence River. Only five years after Columbus's first voyage, Giovanni Caboto, another Italian captain, was the first man to explore North America for King Henry VII of England, who called him John Cabot. By the end of the sixteenth century, England had sent Frobisher, Drake, Hawkins and Gilbert to claim more territories and seek the ever-elusive channel to Asia. Henry Hudson, an Englishman employed by the Dutch, believed that he had found the passage in 1609 when he sailed the *Half Moon* into the river that bears his name.

English, French and Dutch immigrants soon followed these explorers and settled in the colder lands to the north of New Spain. The timber, fish and furs they found there proved to be just as profitable as the Spaniards' gold, though less glamorous. The English were the first to attempt (unsuccessfully, at the start) to send immigrants to populate their territories, although most of the subjects of Good Queen Bess thought it madness that English men and women should consider living in a land of dark forests and hostile savages, three thousand miles from home. Sir Humphrey Gilbert, one of the Queen's versatile soldiers, explored and claimed Newfoundland for England in 1583; he failed to persuade any members of his expedition to remain as farmers on that bleak, foggy island, and one hundred of his potential colonists were drowned in a wreck off Nova Scotia (Gilbert went down with his own ship on the ill-starred journey home). His famous half brother, Sir Walter Raleigh, received a charter from the Queen in 1584 "to discover barbarous countries, not actually possessed of any Christian prince and inhabited by Christian people, to occupy and enjoy the same for ever." Acting immediately to colonize a choice piece of unclaimed land, Raleigh financed an expedition in 1585 of 107 Englishmen to Roanoke Island, off the coast of what later became North Carolina (the entire coastal area, of undefined length, was in those times called Virginia in honor of Raleigh's patron). Finding nothing but frightened Indians and unpromising red earth, these colonists—many of whom were ex-soldiers hoping for a quick and easy fortune—persuaded Sir Francis Drake to convey them back to England the next June. Their tales about the hard winter they had survived—with no women and too few supplies—did not encourage many

"The Arrival of the Englishmen in Virginia" was
drawn by John White, a member of
the first unsuccessful expedition to Roanoke
Island in 1585. This drawing, depicting the
North Carolina coast, was published in De Bry's
edition of A Briefe and True Report of the
New Found Land of Virginia by Thomas Harriot,
another member of the first settlement.
(New York Public Library, Rare Book Division)

other immigrants, but the paintings of Indians and wildlife by one of their party, John White, caused great interest. Raleigh did not give up, but chose his next group of colonists more carefully. Picking eighty-nine men and seventeen women who seemed willing to work the land (each immigrant was offered five hundred acres), he sent them and their eleven children on a second expedition to Roanoke in July, 1587. John White, now the party's leader, sailed back to England to collect more seeds, livestock, iron and cloth, but conflicts with the Spanish Armada caused a fatal delay to his return. When he was able to go back to Roanoke, in August, 1591, all the settlers had vanished, leaving only some storage chests and a name carved on a tree. Not one survivor—or any clue to their fate—was ever found, although remains of a small early fort and a few artifacts unearthed by the National Park Service on Roanoke Island, North Carolina, are believed to indicate the site of the Lost Colony.

The first permanent English settlement in America was established seventeen years later, on May 13, 1607, when the *Godspeed, Discovery* and *Susan Constant* sailed into Chesapeake Bay and up the James River in Virginia. Over a hundred English colonists disembarked and ran into trouble almost immediately. They pitched their tents on an unhealthily low and swampy site, and many of them soon became ill from the salty, slimy drinking water. When they began to erect the palisades of the settlement, which they named Jamestown in honor of their king, it quickly became clear that too many of them were gentlemen-adventurers unused to carpentry, and too few of them were experienced laborers. The settlement was intended to be a trading post, and, in order to satisfy the merchants who sponsored them, the Jamestowners wasted precious weeks prospecting for gold or piling up lumber and iron ore when they should have been growing food to sustain themselves. Incoming ships brought more immigrants instead of food supplies, and that first year the suffering settlers paid dearly for these miscalculations: by September, four months after landing, only forty-six of the original 104 were still alive. Through the winter they lived close to starvation and in terror of the Indians, until "those wild and cruel pagans," as one survivor referred to them, saved the colonists with presents of bread, corn, fish and meat. Sustained by ships bringing more men and supplies, Jamestown then endured the terrible "starving time" of the winter of 1609-1610, when its population was reduced from about five hundred to sixty. The settlement came very close to being permanently abandoned.

Jamestown did endure, however, proving that English men and women could survive and even prosper on the new continent. John Rolfe secured peace by marrying Pocahontas, and laid the basis for future prosperity when he successfully grew and cured tobacco, the "sotweed" that was America's first crop with trading value. More shiploads of immigrants began to arrive, many of them bearing Roman Catholics to the refuge which Lord Baltimore had established in Maryland. Further to the north, in the area named "New England," a thin line of English settlements gradually dotted the coast as far as Maine. Within the large Massachusetts Bay Colony, established in 1630, many towns were founded by Puritans seeking religious freedom—England's "high-church" kings, James I and Charles I, had forbidden them to miss regular Anglican services or to hold unauthorized religious meetings. The new communities grew rapidly. As a series of poor harvests spread hunger across England and the Thirty Years War halted that country's trade with the European continent, some twenty thousand immigrants embarked for New England during what came to be called the Great Migration of 1630 to 1643. Some of the newcomers—Baptists, Presbyterians and Quakers among them—found the uncompromising Puritans of the Massachusetts Bay Colony even less tolerant than the English authorities back home had been. Faced with the choice of absolute conformity or departure, numbers of dissenters moved on to start communities of their own in Rhode Island, New Hampshire and Connecticut. The settling of North America, which by mid-century included about fifty thousand English inhabitants, was well under way.

The Mayflower sailed from Plymouth, England, on September 16, 1620, with 101 passengers and 48 crew crowded aboard. Many of the "Pilgrims" were Puritan separatists from the Church of England who had been living in exile in Holland for over 10 years.

(Library of Congress, Prints & Photographs Division)

In one of the gaps between England's widely scattered northern and southern colonies, the Dutch entrenched themselves in the Hudson River Valley and parts of what became New Jersey. The first few Dutch immigrants landed on Manhattan in May, 1624, two years before the island was purchased from the Indians; they founded Nieuw Amsterdam and other small communities up the river as far as Albany. Vast feudal estates were offered to "patroons" who would bring over fifty immigrants to work the land. But the settlers of New Netherland were by no means all Dutch. When the British seized Nieuw Amsterdam in August, 1664, they were astonished to learn that the inhabitants of the town spoke a total of eighteen different languages—including Swedish, Finnish, French, Portuguese, Spanish, Norwegian, Czech, Danish, Italian, German and Polish.

The national diversity of Nieuw Amsterdam, a foretaste of New York City's future cosmopolitanism, symbolized the way in which immigrants from many parts of the Old World were building colonial America. Far to the north and west of the English colonies, French trappers and traders sparsely inhabited an enormous region from Canada across to Illinois, while down the Mississippi River there were French farmers in Louisiana (named for their Sun King). Their fellow countrymen who were Protestant Huguenots found refuge in many areas of New England (notably Boston) and the South. As early as the first settlement of Jamestown, Italian glass-workers and Polish and German craftsmen had been asked to join the struggling English colonists. The English Quakers, who founded Pennsylvania under the leadership of William Penn, invited German Protestants to join them, and in 1683 the first fourteen German families—forerunners of thousands of Pietists, Mennonites (Amish), Dunkers, Lutherans, Calvinists and Moravians—arrived in the year-old City of Brotherly Love. They were joined by Welsh nationalists who scattered sturdy farmhouses and names like Bryn Mawr across the Pennsylvania countryside. Swedes and Finns established New Sweden around the bay in Delaware, a territory later also granted to Penn. Georgia, granted by a 1732 charter to two English humanitarians, welcomed Jews and fugitive Scottish Highlanders, among others. Some two thousand Jewish immigrants, mainly from Spain and Portugal, found a refuge in America before the Revolution (the first small group fled from Portuguese persecution in Brazil in 1654); many of them settled in Nieuw Amsterdam and in Newport, Rhode Island, where in 1763 they built what is today the oldest synagogue in the country. Meanwhile, out on the frontiers of Pennsylvania, Maryland and the Carolinas, fighting Indians and slowly pushing back the wilderness, were the tough Scotch-Irish—Lowland Presbyterians who had spent several generations farming in northern Ireland, until English pressure drove 200,000 of them to the western spaces of the New World.

By the eve of the Revolution, about 2,500,000 Americans were living in the thirteen colonies—and four out of every ten were not of English origin. (The Germans and their descendants, most thickly settled in Pennsylvania, offered the biggest challenge to the numerical dominance of the English immigrants.) "There is room for everybody in America," wrote the French-born essayist St. John Crevecoeur, and most of the colonists in pre-Revolutionary America, where more strong men were always needed, would have agreed with him. Generally welcoming immigrants of any national origin, America even proved able to assimilate groups as disparate as some fifty thousand of England's unwanted convicts, orphans and paupers, and several hundred French aristocrats, who fled from the Reign of Terror in 1793, built themselves fine mansions in the wilderness and amazed their rustic neighbors with the elegance of their cooking, card parties and cotillions. One of America's complaints in the Declaration of Independence, in fact, was that George III had tried to make it difficult for immigrants to settle in the colonies: "He has endeavoured to prevent the population of these States; for that reason obstructing the Laws for the Naturalization of Foreigners; refusing to pass others to encourage their migrations hither, and raising the conditions of new Appropriations of Lands."

After the war, in which independence was wrested from the British with the aid of commanders such as Lafayette, Kosciusko, Pulaski, Steuben and Rochambeau, the newly autonomous nation opened its gates to the world. During the first decade of independence, only about five thousand immigrants arrived each year. But with the turn of the century and the end of the Napoleonic Wars in Europe in 1815, immigration rapidly accelerated: 150,000 arrived during the 1820's, 1,700,000 in the 1840's, and a staggering 2,500,000 in the 1850's. This so-called wave of immigration brought a total of some five million newcomers to the United States between the Battle of Waterloo and the opening of Castle Garden.

Many of these immigrants were Irish rural laborers fleeing from the devastating potato famines of the 1840's—which killed about one million of their compatriots in five years by disease and outright starvation. At times, it seemed as if the poor and overcrowded southern part of Ireland was virtually emptying itself into the New World. Many English villages, too, sent large numbers of their least fortunate inhabitants to America. The Industrial Revolution in Britain at this time was putting increasing numbers of men out of work, while changes in agriculture were impoverishing thousands of farm laborers. English parish officials quickly realized that paying their paupers' passages to America (at about $40 per adult, $20 for a child) rarely cost more than supporting them at home for one year on the parish allowance. Some European towns emptied their prisons as well as their almshouses by giving every occupant a ticket to New York—where these immigrants often ended up in similar institutions (until an 1882 American law prohibited their entry).

To escape from the despair of poverty, most immigrants left the Old World on their own initiative, and endured almost unbelievable sufferings, risking death itself, on their journey to the land of hope. In a time when poor people never saw newspapers or maps, their only information about the United States might have been a brief letter from an emigrant friend or the tales of some sailor. They leaped into the unknown, with only faith in the future to sustain

The village priest blesses Irish emigrants as they set
out for America. Blight destroyed the potato
crop in 1845 and for the next 3
harvests. One million villagers died from starvation
and disease, while 1,600,000 emigrated in
the 1840's and 1850's, mostly to the United States.
(Illustrated London News, May 10, 1857)

them. In the days when horse-drawn carriages were only for
gentlemen and railroads did not yet exist, they walked
many miles along dusty roads to the nearest port, sometimes pushing their few possessions in a handcart and doing
casual labor for roadside farmers in order to eat. If they
successfully ran the obstacle course of storms, accidents
and thieves, they had to seek out the captain of a sailing
ship bound for an American port and bargain with him for
their passage.

The horrors of the sea voyage itself gave real meaning to
the words of one poor weaver from the west of England,
who in August, 1830, wrote home to his wife: "I would

Salzburgisch

Aug.
Conf.

Arnd
wahr
Chri
thū

Gott ist bey uns in der Noth

Nichts, als das E
Vertreibt uns ins
Verlaßen wir da
So sind wir doch

rche im Winter, oder am Sabbath. Matt 24. v.2

migranten.

...elium
...ilium.
...terland,
...ttes Hand.

BIB...
LIA

This engraving was originally published in 1732
in Johann Michail Teubnern's Complete
History of the Emigrants or Banished Lutherans
from the Archbishopric of Salzburg. As in much
of Europe, Lutherans were persecuted in the Catholic
city of Salzburg. By 1741, about 1,200
Protestant Salzburgers had left for a refuge in
Georgia. The 2 emigrants shown here carry
both the Lutheran Augsburg Confession and the Bible.
(Library of Congress,
Prints & Photographs Division)

rather cross the Atlantic ten times than hear my children cry for victuals once." Fights between passengers and crew were not uncommon, and drunken sailors sometimes looted luggage or attacked unprotected immigrant girls. When the sailing got rough, bewildered villagers were at times ordered to help the sailors man the ship. Andrew Carnegie, a twelve-year-old Scottish lad in 1848 when he sailed on the eight-hundred-ton *Wiscasset* out of Glasgow, recalled in his memoirs: "During the seven weeks of the voyage, I came to know the sailors quite well, learned the names of the ropes, and was able to direct the passengers to answer the call of the boatswain, for the ship being undermanned, the aid of the passengers was urgently required." On many ships, immigrants were put under the command of the second mate, who ordered them to help in the galley, swab the decks, empty the chamber pots or wash dirty laundry. The most unfortunate of the immigrants sailed on ships that never made it—ships that foundered due to storms, rocks, mutinies or (in spite of the ban on matches and candles in steerage) disastrous fires.

Hunger and thirst were primary dangers on the small sailing vessels which took from four to fourteen weeks—or longer—to make the transatlantic crossing. Fickle winds meant the journey was always unpredictable. (Sailing brigs in the 1840's generally took nine or ten weeks to cross from Ireland, while the fastest ships out of Bremen in the next decade averaged six weeks.) Many captains, particularly on English and French ships, required passengers to provide their own food, as well as cooking utensils, water containers and bedding. One experienced English seaman, publishing his advice to emigrants in 1832, recommended that they take sixty days' worth of the following: bacon, biscuit, butter, tea, sugar, oatmeal, flour, barley (for making broth), pepper, mustard, pickled onions, pickled tripe, cheese and a small bottle of peppermint essence for use "when the children are a little qualmish." Even when the ship's stores provided such food as biscuit and salt beef (which the above mariner described as "generally very unpleasant"), each family of immigrants was expected to cook its own meals, often on small brick-lined coal fires at each side of the foredeck. Only on the first day at sea was the meat and bread issued from the galley really fresh; after two weeks without refrigeration, unsalted meat was rotten, butter rancid, and the travelers' unhealthy diet consisted largely of dried herring, potatoes, prunes, thin barley soup, weak coffee and brackish drinking water to which more and more vinegar had to be added as the weeks passed. On sailing ships transporting ten or twelve pampered passengers in first-class cabins on the upper deck, there might be cows, pigs and chickens aboard to provide fresh milk, meat and eggs—and crates of champagne to serve as a tonic. But the unhappy souls down in steerage received no such luxuries, and they became ill with diarrhea, trenchmouth and scurvy. One out of ten died.

The mortality rates on these "coffin ships" would have been high even with the best diet available, because of the terrible overcrowding, dirt and lack of ventilation. European laws did exist to limit the number of passengers a sailing ship might carry, but enterprising captains would load the permitted number of people at their main port of departure, then sail to another harbor, where a hundred more unfortunates might be crammed into steerage. So-called because it was near the steering apparatus, the steerage deck was below the main deck and not far above the hold, usually near the stern. It was dark, windowless and usually no more than 5½ feet high. On both sides of narrow aisles, immigrants were squeezed side by side onto "bunks" which were merely rough wooden platforms covered with straw. Belongings had to be stacked in the aisles. In the widest passageway was a crude wooden table, sometimes so small that only a quarter of the steerage passengers could have their meals at it, while the rest ate on deck or (in bad weather) crouched in the gangways. The only daylight and fresh air filtered into steerage through overhead hatches and when storms struck, these were closed, sometimes for many days, while immigrants were forbidden to go up on deck for even their normal hour or two a day. The scene in steerage during the worst Atlantic storms was hellish: as the small ship plunged through heavy seas, waves smashed against the hollow-sounding bow and sent rattling showers of spray against the deck overhead, while the imprisoned immigrants screamed as they were flung about in their bunks. When the swaying lantern sputtered out, they were left in utter darkness, and most of them prayed as if their last hour had come.

The storms and sickness were too terrible to recall easily, but impossible ever to forget. One woman from a Sussex village wrote to her parents after landing in New York in May, 1828: "I often look back upon the scenes that we have passed through. While we were passing over the water our sufferings were great; but that God that is loving to all

One of the earliest pictures of immigrants in steerage, published in 1851, was drawn at the beginning of the decade that saw 2,500,000 newcomers land in the United States. Sailing ships in these years crossed to Europe

them that trust in Him, has brought us through. I will not grieve your hearts with all our sufferings, for my paper will not hold it. Little Mary was very ill with the fever that so many died with,—7 children and one woman; to hear their cries and moans, it was very bad. I was so ill myself, that I was forced to crawl out of my bed, and lay on the floor while John made the bed. If you know of any coming here, tell them never to come where the vessel is so full; for we was shut down in darkness for a fortnight, till so many died; then the hatch was opened. I will not grieve your poor hearts with more about what we poor creatures suffered. I

heavily laden with American cargoes of tobacco, cotton, rice or timber. For the west-bound journey, temporary flooring and bunks were installed in the 'tween-decks, and immigrants were crammed in to capacity—as profitable ballast.
(*Illustrated London News, May 10, 1851*)

African slaves were unwilling immigrants to
America for over 250 years. On ships like the
Gloria, illustrated here from Drake's *Revelations
of a Slave Smuggler* (1856), they were
chained in pairs for voyages that lasted over
3 months, during which 1 out of 5 died.
*(Library of Congress, Prints &
Photographs Division)*

cannot tell you what day of the month we landed into New York; but we was about 33 days coming over, which was called a good passage."

On slave ships, the slaves were kept on the 'tween-decks, as the steerage area was called, and immigrants on the very worst sailing vessels fared little better than slaves—on some notorious English ships transporting Irish peasants, almost a quarter of the passengers died. Sailors in many ports boasted that they could always tell an immigrant ship, without inquiring what the cargo was, by its stink. As late as 1854, when conditions had been much improved on the larger and faster clipper ships, one out of every six immigrants still became dangerously ill or died at sea, and an inquiry authorized by Congress revealed that 25 per cent of the immigrant ships arriving from London had cases of cholera aboard. The year before this investigation, when the *Howard* had docked after a fourteen-week crossing from Hamburg, thirty-seven of her 286 passengers were dead of cholera, and more than a third of the survivors had been too weak to move from their bunks; they had had no decent drinking water for forty-two days. The investigating committee, headed by Hamilton Fish, recommended a law that would make it illegal for any passengers to sleep (as on crowded ships they occasionally did) on the "orlop" deck below steerage: the orlop deck, which could not be washed for fear of damaging the cargo just beneath it, was frequently overrun with rats from the hold, and it received no direct daylight or air at all.

As early as March 2, 1819, Congress had passed one law to help more of the immigrants reach the New World alive and in reasonable health. On ships arriving in American ports, the government decreed, no more than two passengers could be transported for every five tons of the vessel's capacity. Every captain, moreover, was to give to customs officials in the port of arrival a list of the immigrants on his ship—describing their age, sex, occupation, where they came from and where they were going—and a report on those who had died during the crossing. Finding that the law discriminated against the lightweight but fast sailing ships built in America, in 1847 Congress

The first transatlantic steamships—such
as the Liverpool, shown here on her first voyage
to New York in October, 1838—were
equipped with 30-foot paddle wheels (and sails
in case the engines failed). The Liverpool's crossings
averaged 20 days, and she carried only rich
passengers. But as improvements were devised and
fares dropped, steamships began to compete for
the poorer immigrant's patronage around 1860.
Sailing-ship owners hastily improved their
steerage quarters, but by the 1870's
their business was ruined by the faster ships.

(Library of Congress,
Prints & Photographs Division)

69

Steamships (with auxiliary sails) began to carry immigrants around 1860. But even on the newest vessels, the journey was still dangerous. The White Star liner Atlantic, sailing from Liverpool to New York in April, 1873, ran short of coal and changed course for Halifax. Going at full

speed, the 3,700-ton steamer struck Golden
Rule Rock off the coast of Nova Scotia and sank
in less than 15 minutes—562 of the 952 people
on board were drowned. Currier and Ives published
this memorial lithograph later that year.
(Library of Congress,
Prints & Photographs Division)

amended it to relate to the ship's interior space rather than tonnage: for every passenger there must be fourteen square feet of horizontal space (twenty-two square feet if the steerage ceiling was lower than five feet), and the minimum size for a berth was to be 6 by 1½ feet.

With no federal officials to enforce it, the law was not strictly observed. But its enactment did put an end to the scandalous overcrowding that had been common during the eighteenth century on ships carrying a class of immigrants known as "redemptioners." It has been estimated that over half of all the white immigrants who landed in colonial America arrived as indentured servants, bound to work from four to seven years for the master who had paid their passage. The redemptioners were the unluckiest of this group. Not having any specific American employers waiting for them, redemptioners signed their indentures over to their ships' captains; they "redeemed" their unpaid passages when the captains auctioned these papers to the highest bidders in the ports of arrival. The redemptioners were no more able to choose their masters or object to the conditions of their servitude than slaves, and they were severely punished for running away. To make matters worse, many of them landed in America to find themselves obligated for much longer servitude than the few years specified on their indentures. For, just before their ships sailed, many captains made them sign another agreement: in case of deaths at sea, the surviving redemptioners would have to work out the terms of those who had died, as well as their own. Since the captains made these voyages profitable by packing redemptioners into steerage as closely as slaves, forcing them to sleep in the gangways as well as the bunks, it was not rare for one out of three of these immigrants to die at sea, and the survivors were expected to work in bondage for virtually the rest of their lives. It was a blessing to the poor of Europe when the American laws on over-crowding made the system unprofitable for ship owners.

Except for insisting that arriving immigrants be counted, and that it was inhuman to crowd them beyond a certain point, the American government left control of immigration largely to the individual states until 1875 (the year in which it banned criminals and prostitutes from entry). The local authorities worried at first about only one problem: the danger that boatloads of unwashed and unhealthy immigrants might carry smallpox, typhoid fever or cholera through the streets of the cities where they disembarked. Quarantine was therefore the main screening process through which the earliest immigrants had to pass. As they clustered on deck in the harbor, a local health inspector scanned them quickly for signs of contagious illnesses, examined the ship's records for details of deaths at sea, then allowed the vessel to anchor by the docks. In New York, passengers and sailors who were found to be suffering from one of the dreaded diseases were sent to the Marine Hospital on Staten Island's eastern shore, which was founded in 1797 and financed after 1830 by a head tax on arriving immigrants—the city's Health Commissioner collected $1.50 for the captain and each cabin-class passenger, $1.00 for each steerage passenger and sailor.

As the number of immigrants continued to rise every year, and America's cities became increasingly crowded, other questions were asked. For one thing, New York (like

Overleaf: Immigrants who reached an American
port safely—like these disembarking
from the packet ship Kossuth in New York
in 1851—found their troubles were not
over, between claiming their baggage, looking for
friends or finding their way unaided to the
train or riverboat. Strangers who offered help in their
own language often turned out to be
thieves. This woodcut was published in Gleason's
Pictorial Drawing-Room Companion, June 14, 1851.
*(Library of Congress,
Prints & Photographs Division)*

COSSOUTH.

every other state along the coast from Maine to Florida where immigrants were landing) wanted to ensure that newcomers would not become beggars or paupers to add to the cities' problems. In some states, immigrants were occasionally asked to post bonds as a guarantee that they would never need public charity, but most newcomers arrived with so little money that this scheme never worked. In the end, a simple admission tax was usually levied on each person.

Immigrants who arrived safely and prospered in the New World never forgot the horrors of their journey, and they tried to make sure that the same sufferings would not be inflicted on their countrymen who followed. The German and the Irish Emigrant Societies were established in 1784 and 1841 respectively, to protect newcomers of these nationalities. These two organizations overcame considerable opposition in persuading the legislators of New York State to create a Board of Commissioners of Emigration, which finally came into being on May 5, 1847. Six of the board's members were appointed by the governor, while the other four were the mayors of New York City and Brooklyn and the presidents of the Irish and German Emigrant Societies. Their first accomplishment in 1847 was the establishment of the Emigrant Hospital and Refuge on Ward's Island in the East River, where immigrants suffering from noncontagious illnesses could be cared for. The Marine Hospital was simultaneously placed under the new board's control.

The commissioners had plenty of other problems to worry about. Shipping lines throughout the nineteenth century used New York as the principal port for discharging immigrants, in preference to Boston, Philadelphia, Baltimore or New Orleans. Always the busiest harbor on the eastern seaboard for this reason, New York, in 1848, was suddenly busier than it had ever been before. In that year there was an abortive revolution in Germany, led by liberals and nationalists who were easily suppressed by the authorities. Thousands of disillusioned political exiles, many of them intellectual leaders like Carl Schurz, joined the stream of Irish, English and Scandinavian immigrants sailing into

New York harbor in search of a new life. The statistics of arrivals in the port rose to unprecedented heights. In 1848, the harassed commissioners reported, 189,176 immigrants landed in the city. In 1850, disembarking from 1,912 ships, 212,796 newcomers arrived—117,038 Irishmen, 45,535 Germans and 50,223 others. Harbor inspectors were soon no longer able to look at all the immigrants and check the papers on board all the anchored vessels that clogged the port. The established ethnic benevolent societies complained loudly, in the meantime, that helpless newcomers were being swindled and robbed on the waterfront as soon as they disembarked. Since ships discharged their passengers at docks covering three to four miles of the East and "North" (or Hudson) river banks, neither these societies not the police could cover the area well enough to keep a protective watch over all the immigrants, who had to fend off marauders the minute the gangplank went down.

The worst of the thieves were the boarding-house "runners" who lured immigrants to decrepit lodgings run by their predatory countrymen. If an immigrant hesitated too long, the runner would add force to his argument by seizing a valuable box of tools, the baby, or the wrist of the prettiest daughter, and making off through the crowd at top speed. The immigrant and his family were forced to follow. The boarding house they reached would be run by someone who spoke their language and who would inveigle them into staying on for several days—at a charge three or four times higher than the first day's rate. Outrageous charges for transporting or storing baggage were also added to the bill. If the immigrant could not or would not pay, he was turned penniless into the street while his belongings were held as "security." When this practice was outlawed, the immigrant's luggage was often "stolen" with the proprietor's connivance. Often terrified of the police because of his experiences in Europe, the immigrant knew no one to whom he could turn for help.

The time had clearly come, the commissioners and the ethnic societies agreed, to open a centralized receiving station where all immigrants could be properly inspected, protected from thieves and directed on their way.

III
Castle
Garden
[1855-1890]

The place chosen as New York's first immigrant receiving station was a fifty-year-old circular fort, originally known as Castle Clinton in the anxious days when its twenty-eight guns stood ready to defend Manhattan against possible British invasion. Renamed Castle Garden when its military use ended, it had been elegantly remodelled and fitted with six thousand seats in front of a large stage. For the last fifteen years, New York's fashionable ladies and gentlemen had flocked to the waterfront "resort" to hear band concerts and operas, to watch acrobats, balloon ascensions and fireworks, and—most fabulous of all—to cheer Jenny Lind, the Swedish Nightingale, at her American debut. By the time the theater managers' last lease expired in 1854, however, fashionable New York had begun to move uptown, and Castle Garden's days as a place of entertainment were over.

Because it had been built to command the harbor, the

This bird's-eye view of Castle Garden, a circular fort at the southwest tip of Manhattan, shows it in 1855, when it was first used for immigrants.
(*Illustrated London News, November 24, 1855*)

Castle Garden's external appearance changed as
land was filled in around the old causeway
and additional outbuildings were erected
by the Commissioners of Emigration of the
State of New York. This engraving appeared in a
French magazine, L'Univers Illustré, in October, 1869.
(New York Public Library, Picture Collection)

old fort extended far out into the water and could be easily
approached by ferry boats. It was big, it was solidly
constructed, it was owned by the city. It was, obviously,
the ideal place for an immigrants' depot. But the frustrated
Commissioners of Emigration were not free to bid for it
until the New York State Legislature approved of the idea.
The needed authorization was finally granted on April 13,
1855. After negotiations with civic authorities, the lease
was transferred to the commissioners for four years as of
May 5, 1855.

Difficulties were not over, however. Many of the thirty
thousand citizens of the First Ward, in which Castle Garden
stood, were horrified. They complained that the daily
crowds of baggage-laden immigrants would inconvenience
respectable citizens doing business on Broadway; 530
merchants signed a petition to ban the depot. Mr. Lorenzo

Delmonico feared that the prosperity of his hotel at 25 Broadway would suffer. House owners (including Cornelius Vanderbilt, residing in a $35,000 mansion at 5 Bowling Green) foresaw that the prevailing summer winds would blow "pestilential and disagreeable odors" into their windows, forcing residents to leave and driving property values down. Many residents were nervous about epidemics. Editors of the *New-York Daily Times* suggested that the best thing to do with Castle Garden was demolish it, since it was only a nuisance and obstructed the park's view of the harbor. The newly enlarged Battery Park, they said, would become a lounging place for immigrants and riffraff if the depot was opened there.

The commissioners promised to enclose Castle Garden with a high board fence, isolating it from the park and leaving it accessible only by water (an impractical promise and one that was never kept). They would not use Castle Garden as a lodging or "victualling house" for immigrants, and so deprive local merchants of business. They produced reputable physicians to testify that the danger of epidemics would be reduced if immigrants were examined before being released into the city's streets. All these arguments swayed Judge Hoffman of the Superior Court, and he ordered a temporary injunction removed on June 8, 1855.

Extensive repairs were needed, but they were done quickly, and on August 1, 1855, Castle Garden was officially opened as America's first receiving station for immigrants.

The first three ships cleared quarantine and discharged immigrants at Castle Garden on Friday, August 3. These were the forerunners of some eight million immigrants who would enter here between 1855 and 1890. When the immigrants saw Castle Garden, all of its lavish decorations were gone. The once elegant "refreshment rooms" near the main entrance were converted into functional bathrooms, with rows of basins and towels, and huge twenty-foot tubs with continuously running water. The seats on the floor were replaced by plain wooden benches, leaving most of the area empty for the crowds of people who would be surging around central desks marked—for those who could read

English—"Registry," "General Information," "Exchange Office" and "Railroad Department." Where the famous stage had stood, an iron staircase rose to the "Office of Commissioners of Emigration, General Agent & Superintendent," and uniformed men with papers in their hands ran briskly up and down the stairs with ringing footsteps. Outside, billboards that had once featured Jenny Lind now advertised "Labor Exchange," "Ward's Island Department" and "Entrance for Emigrants Only."

Immigrants who landed at Castle Garden received a warm welcome compared to their predecessors. The system at the new receiving station was by no means perfect, but officials did their best to register immigrants quickly, and help them to exchange money, buy railroad tickets, transport baggage and find a job or a place to stay. Immigrants were now given initial protection, at least, from waiting swindlers and thieves, "depredators being limited," in the words of one commissioner, "to fellow passengers." Compared to the former free-for-all on the docks, the commissioners claimed, newcomers were now "enabled to depart for their future homes without having their means impaired, their morals corrupted, and probably their persons diseased." The immigrants themselves certainly appreciated the improvement and spread the news to their compatriots. When the receiving station had been in operation for nearly twenty years, the *New-York Times* (February 27, 1874) reported: "Castle Garden is so well known in Europe that few emigrants can be induced to sail for any other destination. Their friends in this country write to those who are intending to emigrate to come to Castle Garden where they will be safe, and, if out of money, they can remain until it is sent to them. Complaints are frequently received by the commissioners from emigrants who have been landing at Halifax or Boston, though they were promised to be brought to New York. Thus emigrant-runners abroad seek steerage passengers even by deception." Deceptions were sometimes practiced on a broader scale, as was discovered by several dozen families from Pilsen, Bohemia, who asked a Hamburg agent in 1863 to send them to Nebraska—they landed in New Zealand.

Immigrants sailing to New York benefited from other improvements which stemmed from new legislation passed in the year of Castle Garden's opening. As a result of the 1854 Senate inquiry into the deplorable "causes and the extent of the sickness and mortality prevailing on board the emigrant ships," the passenger laws were stiffened on March 3, 1855. New rules specified the proportion of passengers to tonnage, the space to be allowed for each passenger on board, discipline, cleanliness, ventilation and food and cooking provisions. Every ship bringing aliens to America was now required to supply a complete manifest of its

Castle Garden's interior, drawn for Harper's in 1871, was as crowded as ever. The floor of the rotunda was divided into separate areas for English-speaking immigrants (mainly Irish) and others, and was estimated to hold anywhere from 2,000 to 4,000 people. *(New York Public Library, Picture Collection)*

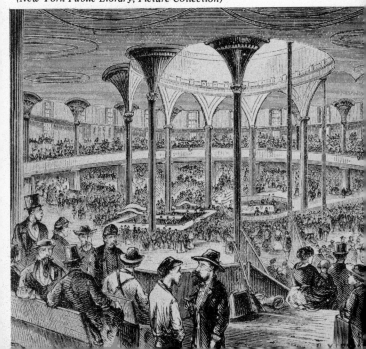

On the deck of a sailing ship in the 1870's,
immigrants scan the horizon for their
first glimpse of America. At this time old
sailing vessels still took 6 weeks or more to cross
the Atlantic. By 1875, most immigrants
landing at Castle Garden came on steamships,
which were faster—but still often crowded and dirty.
Drawn for Every Saturday, May 6, 1871.
(New York Public Library, Picture Collection)

84

passengers to the local customs collectors, who would then pass on the list to the federal government. These laws remained in effect for nearly thirty years.

In spite of all the changes for the better, the experience of reaching New York was still exhausting, frightening and often dangerous. When Castle Garden opened as a depot, 95 per cent of the immigrants arrived on old sailing ships which took an unpredictable number of weeks to make the crossing. They were smaller and less comfortable than the early steamships, on which about half the immigrants traveled by the mid-1870's. One English immigrant, who spent seven weeks in 1863 on a sailing vessel he called an "old tub" (the *City of London*), recorded in his memoirs the lack of space and comfort: "We had none of the modern comforts of travel. The sleeping quarters were cramped and we had to do our own cooking in the galley of the boat. Mother had provided salt beef and other preserved meats and fish, dried vegetables, and red pickled cabbage which I remember most vividly. We were all seasick except father, mother the longest of all. Father had to do the cooking in the meanwhile and take care of the sick. . . . Father didn't know much about cooking. I remember his experience with split peas. He put three quarts of peas in the kettle with a corresponding amount of water. When the water began to boil and the peas to swell, he had to keep on adding water until the peas became soft. Such oceans of peas—peas in all kinds of containers—peas everywhere. For days we ate peas and pea soup."

If the ship was badly run, conditions could be dreadful. Seventy Germans who sailed from Le Havre on the badly overcrowded *Atalanta* in October, 1865, sent a bitter letter to New York's German-language newspaper, describing the horrors of their journey: they were served no food at all their first day on board, then only one meal every twenty-four hours; the steerage was filthy and reeked of calcium chloride; warm water had to be paid for; one man paid twenty francs to get soup for his sick family but never received it; by the time the ship's doctor condescended to visit the sick in steerage, many were already dead. The crossing was unimaginably worse for the German families who came two years later on the sailing ship *Leibnitz* from Hamburg. Head winds forced the ship through the tropics, and when it landed in New York on January 11, 1868, after a voyage of fourteen weeks, 108 of the 544 passengers were dead. The ship was the filthiest the boarding officer in New York had ever seen: the upper of the two steerage decks had only two hatchways for ventilation, and the orlop deck was, in his words, "a perfect pesthole, calculated to kill the healthiest man." It was so dark that one could see no farther than three feet, its air so foul that lanterns would hardly burn, and it reeked of bilge water and excrement. There had not been enough food or fresh water. There was no doctor on board, and the ship's medicine chest had been emptied after only two weeks at sea. When the first deaths had occurred, the corpses were left in steerage for twenty-four hours and were covered with vermin when finally tossed overboard. The Public Health Service doctors who boarded the ship in quarantine reported that the passengers had died of "intestinal catarrh" and typhoid fever. At Castle Garden many of the surviving young children, when asked where their parents were, pointed to the ocean and sobbed, "Down there."

Fire was a hazard on all ships, and in 1866 the disastrous burning of the *William Nelson* at sea caused the deaths of 426 immigrants. The most conscientious captain could do nothing about the fierce gales that sometimes whipped the Atlantic, and to seasick villagers who had spent their lives inland, a storm at sea was a terrifying sight from the deck of a small ship. One Serbian boy, crossing the Atlantic during the March storms of 1874, later remembered watching, "through the howling darkness, the white rims of the mountain-high waves speeding on like maddened dragons toward the tumbling ship . . . ."

Below deck, steerage was always uncomfortable, even when the sea was calm. One young man, who came from Russia as late as 1895, described the immigrants' quarters as "a large egg crate, with three tiers of cubicles for bunks and with just enough room in the center to move about before climbing in and out of our beds." Even on clean ships, the overcrowding, stale air, odors of disinfectants and lack of

**The liners Egypt and Spain of the National
Steamship Line passing each other between
New York and Liverpool in 1879.**
*(Library of Congress,
Prints & Photographs Division)*

hot soapy water made all clothes and possessions stink for
months after landing. The same young Russian, who
estimated that the smell took a year to wear off, recorded
"an olfactory phenomenon known to all transatlantic
travelers of those days as the smell of 'ship.' This pervasive,
insidious odor," he wrote, "a distillation of bilge and a
number of less identifiable putrescences, settled on one's
person, clothes, and luggage and stayed there forever,
impervious to changes of habitat, clothing, and the cleans-
ing agents available to the poor. It was many years before I
realized that only steerage passengers smelled of 'ship.' . . .
One *expected* arrivals from Europe to smell of 'ship.' So
much so that on visits to the homes of neighbors, one could
tell at once by the pervading smell of 'ship' that they were
entertaining guests from abroad."

In spite of dangers and discomforts, the human tide kept
coming in. In 1881, over 455,600 immigrants passed
through Castle Garden, more than double the average

annual rate in the past. The following year the record was broken again (not to be surpassed until 1903) as 476,000 arrived. Almost 70 per cent of all immigrants arriving in the United States were landing at Castle Garden.

The old rules, like the old buildings, became inadequate. On August 3, 1882, the federal government finally took action and passed the first comprehensive national immigration law. Under the terms of this Act to Regulate Immigration, state-run boards, under contract to the Secretary of the Treasury, were to inspect immigrants according to rules that were uniform in all ports. Undesirable aliens were to be kept out of the country. Local inspectors were forbidden to admit any prostitutes, Chinese "coolies" or "any convict, lunatic, idiot or any person unable to take care of himself or herself without becoming a public charge." Shipping lines were to pay fifty cents per immigrant to cover the costs of administering landing depots and hospitals. In 1883, the New York State Commissioners of Emigration signed a contract with the federal government to continue operating Castle Garden under these terms.

In the final ten years of Castle Garden's use as a depot, almost 5,250,000 immigrants landed in American ports, and the majority of them—over 3,780,000—came to New York. The decade was not half over before everyone realized that the old fort could no longer be stretched to handle such numbers. Cabin-class passengers were inspected while their ship was sailing up the bay from quarantine, so that the well-to-do (and many "undesirable" aliens who knew the system) avoided detailed questions and physical examinations. But the fact that these passengers did not pass through Castle Garden made no noticeable difference to the overstrained facilities there.

Thieves and unlicensed "runners" still waited to trap unwary immigrants outside the gates, in spite of the commissioners' best efforts to banish them from Castle Garden. There was also trouble up the river at Ward's Island, where sick immigrants were confined in the hospital, next to the Refuge for the destitute. Occasional riots broke out on that island. Some immigrants actually leaped into the East River and swam to Manhattan, begging the police

Russian and Polish immigrants on the Victoria, in
quarantine in April, 1881, objected violently
when the New York State health inspectors,
always fearing epidemics, boarded their ship
and insisted on vaccinating them.
*(Library of Congress,
Prints & Photographs Division)*

to lock them up in city jails, instead. They told tall stories that turned out to have some truth in them—the infirm were shut up with the insane, there wasn't enough food and the bodies of immigrants who died were often used for medical dissection. The death rate was high.

Complaints about the way the commissioners ran Castle Garden had been made regularly over the years, often by citizens whose political or commercial interests clashed with those of the depot. There had been charges of political patronage, excessive profits from the sale of railroad tickets and abusive behavior by employees. In 1883, New York's Governor Grover Cleveland referred, rather unjustly some felt, to "unblushing peculation," and announced that "the present management of this very important department is a scandal and a reproach to civilization." A few years later, Joseph Pulitzer's *World* (July 27, 1887) called the commission "a cumbrous and unwieldy institution" in which no responsibility could be pinned on anyone.

Washington thought it was time to investigate. The Secretary of the Treasury authorized an inquiry in August, 1887, and the following year Congressional and Senatorial committees held investigations of their own. Not surprisingly, they found that Castle·Garden's facilities were hopelessly inadequate for the daily flow of immigrants, and that local inspectors were unable to enforce the simple rules: "large numbers of persons not lawfully entitled to land in the United States are annually received at this port." Missionaries testified that they had seen immigrants forced to sleep overnight on wooden benches or the bare floor. Other abuses were due to greed: some immigrants were

Overleaf: Ships anchored near Castle Garden and, after customs officers had inspected baggage on board, 2 150-ton barges ferried immigrants to this dock.
(*Frank Leslie's Illustrated Newspaper*, November 23, 1878)

A clerk registered immigrants at a desk in Castle
Garden's main rotunda after they had passed
medical inspection. He asked each immigrant's
name, nationality, former residence and intended
destination. Drawn for Harper's, March, 1871.
(New York Public Library, Picture Collection)

made to pay twice for shipment of their baggage. The
railroads, it was revealed, were making enormous amounts
of money from ticket sales, while money-changers were
giving rates less favorable than the true market rate. One of
the New York State Commissioners summed things up
when he frankly told the House of Representatives that
Castle Garden's operation was "a perfect farce."

New York was not the only port for which the Treasury
Department reported "grave difficulties in the execution of
the law." Immigrants were landing at the ports of Portland
(Maine), Boston, Philadelphia, Baltimore, Key West, New
Orleans, Galveston and San Francisco, some of which were
reluctant to hand over to Washington all the revenue from

the new fifty-cent head tax. The Secretary of the Treasury firmly recommended that the federal government take over from the states the whole business of admitting immigrants to the country.

The government's contract with New York's Commissioners of Emigration was terminated as of April 18, 1890. The last immigrants to pass through Castle Garden, on that day, were a group of 465 off the steamers *Bohemia* and *State of Indiana*. Then Castle Garden closed its doors. No one in authority would attempt to introduce an efficient system of receiving immigrants in a place with such a reputation. For six years, the old fort was dark and silent. In 1896 it opened once again in its former role as a place for public amusement, this time as the municipal aquarium. On opening day more than thirty thousand people flocked in to stare at its wonders of aquatic life, and millions of New Yorkers came over the next forty-five years, crowding the great floor and staring at whales, seals, sharks and porpoises splashing in oval tubs. Closed in 1940 to make room for the construction of the Brooklyn-Battery Tunnel, the aquarium moved to Coney Island. The old fort of Castle Clinton was declared a national monument in 1950.

The immigrants kept on arriving, of course, but they were now under the supervision of the new Federal Bureau of Immigration (named, with proper American emphasis, for people who were immigrating into the United States rather than emigrating out of Europe). While it looked for a better place, the bureau received immigrants for two years, 1890 to 1891, in the Barge Office and its annex, a landing place in the Battery Park close to Castle Garden.

Government officials arrived in New York on March 21, 1890, to survey the harbor for a site on which to build a new receiving station. An island seemed best—there newcomers could be protected from swindlers at the gates, and could more easily be transported to railroad terminals in New Jersey. The Secretary of the Treasury had cast an acquisitive eye earlier at twelve-acre Bedloe's Island, conveniently close to the New Jersey shore. He had been defeated by an outcry from New Yorkers who did not want any "Babel" there to detract from their new marvel, the

This cheery scene was described by the artist as "a national dance"—its nationality apparently too complex to define. Of the 8 million immigrants who entered through Castle Garden, most were German (3,425,000) and Irish (2,541,000). The rest, in descending numerical

Statue of Liberty Enlightening the World, which had been unveiled by President Grover Cleveland only four years before. When word reached sculptor Auguste Bartholdi in Paris that an immigration station might be built next to his statue, he was horrified, and criticized the "monstrous plan" as "desecration." The immigration officials next eyed Governor's Island, but military officers adamantly opposed handing over any of their choice space to the immigrants.

The citizens of New Jersey, meanwhile, were petitioning the federal government to remove an old naval powder magazine from a smaller island which they thought was dangerously close to their shore. This was Ellis Island—a tiny low-lying islet of mud and sand in shallow water, north

order, were English, Swedish, Italian, Scottish,
Russian, Norwegian, Swiss, French, Hungarian,
Danish, Austrian, Dutch, Bohemian,
Welsh, Belgian, Spanish, Polish, Chinese,
Portuguese, Greek, Turkish and
Australian . . . plus 162,173 from "other countries."
(Culver Pictures)

of the much larger Bedloe's Island. In Congress that
January, Senator John McPherson of New Jersey had
sponsored a joint resolution authorizing the Secretary of
the Navy to remove the explosives from the Island, and to
purchase some safer site for the naval magazines. No one,
not even the navy, wanted Ellis Island for any other
purpose. The government already owned it. The conclusion
was inevitable. The members of the Joint Committee on
Immigration stopped sailing around the harbor, returned to
Washington and (with only two opposing votes) approved
the selection of Ellis Island as the site for the new
immigration station. President Benjamin Harrison signed
the McPherson bill into law on April 11, 1890.

IV
Ellis Island's
Early Years
[Before 1907]

The 1890 law authorizing removal of the navy's powder magazine from Ellis Island carried an important amendment—an appropriation of $75,000 "to enable the Secretary of the Treasury to improve said Ellis Island for immigration purposes." The citizens of New Jersey were delighted to be rid of the explosives. Everyone seemed pleased, in fact, except the man who had to build the immigrant receiving station.

The Secretary of the Treasury had taken a quick look at Ellis Island earlier that year and dismissed it as an impossible place on which to build anything. The water around it was so shallow that the small revenue cutter he was on could get no closer than 150 yards. The Island itself was so

With its 4 "picturesque" towers,
blue slate roof, buff-painted wooden walls and rows
of gleaming windows, the first station on Ellis Island
looked to 1 journalist like a modern "watering-place
hotel." About 400 feet by 150 feet, the
main building was larger than the original Island,
which had been doubled in area by landfill.
Photographed soon after its completion in January, 1892,
by J.W. Johnson, View & Marine Photo, N.Y.
(Brown Brothers)

low, he informed the Joint Committee on Immigration, that "it seemed to be almost on a level with the water." He had ordered the boat to turn back, and had, he said, "steamed away from it under the impression that even if we could get rid of the powder magazine which is there now, and could secure the island, it was not a desirable place; and we were so advised by the collector of customs of New York and some others who were with us."

Desirable or not, Ellis Island was the site on which the Sectrary of the Treasury had to build and operate the first federal immigration depot, and there was nothing he could do about it.

The ghosts of many generations of New Yorkers, long since dead when the secretary faced his problem, would have agreed with him that the Island was not a very desirable or accessible place. The Indians had called it Kioshk, or Gull Island, after the birds that were its only inhabitants. It was nothing more than a small sandbank, consisting of about three acres of soft mud and clay, so low that it barely rose above the high tide level of the Upper Bay. Together with a now-submerged reef and its larger neighbor (later called Bedloe's or Liberty Island), it was part of the group of Oyster Islands in the shallow waters off the New Jersey shore. Its sands were mixed with oyster shells which attracted the gulls and, later, fishermen who used the Island as a place from which to stake out nets during the spring run of shad.

This small mudbank, purchased in 1630 from the Indians by the governors of Nieuw Amsterdam, had been known by many names during the previous 250 years. Dutch fishermen had called it Little Oyster Island. As it passed through the hands of various owners in British colonial times, it was renamed Dyre's, then Bucking, Island. A more sinister name—Gibbet Island—dated from the 1760's, when the first of several pirates to be executed there was hanged from a gibbet or gallows tree. At the time of the American Revolution, the Island was in the hands of the owner, whose name finally stuck to it: Samuel Ellis, dealer in general merchandise (spars for masts or bowsprits, barrels of excellent shad and herrings, cheap twine, even a nearly-new Pleasure Sleigh) and landlord of a small tavern on the Island catering to fishermen. Ellis tried without luck to sell what he still called Oyster Island, but his heirs successfully sold it (for a cool $10,000) to the government on the eve of the War of 1812.

As a piece of real estate, the Island, barely one hundred yards long, was not at all desirable: it lacked good fresh water, and its clay soil was too soft to support any heavy buildings without landfill. But cannon mounted on it could be combined with the newly installed guns on Bedloe's and Governor's islands to form an impenetrable crossfire for defending Manhattan. The only military action on the Island, however, happened in 1814, when a soldier was executed for trying to murder his officer. The army and navy both made slight use of the Island and its small fort as the years passed. In 1835 the navy began storing ammunition there—the start of the "powder magazine" which by the 1880's was causing a public furor among the anxious residents of nearby New Jersey.

In 1890, after the McPherson bill was signed, the powder was moved to Fort Wadsworth on the Narrows on May 24, 1890. In the New York offices of the Superintendent of Repairs of United States Buildings, planning for the immigrant receiving station got under way. To make the small, muddy Island usable, every penny of that $75,000 was going to be needed.

First, a channel 1,250 feet long and 200 feet wide had to be dredged to a depth of 12 feet or more and new docks constructed so that ferryboats could approach and land passengers at the Island. The second problem, as the army had discovered over eighty years earlier, was that the Island wasn't big enough for any substantial building. The government's engineers solved that by doubling its area with landfill held in place by 860 feet of surrounding cribwork. There wasn't enough fresh water, so artesian wells and cisterns had to be dug. Under the supervision of Major

The interior walls of the first station on Ellis Island
were finished in natural wood, as shown in
this drawing of the detention area from Harper's
Weekly in 1893. This huge firetrap burned
completely on June 14, 1897, only 5½ years
after its completion.
(Harper's Weekly, August 26, 1893)

George B. Hibbard, the contractors Sheridan & Byrne then
went to work on the new buildings, which had been
designed by a government architect.

New Yorkers strolling in Battery Park and crossing the
Hudson River on ferries watched with interest as the great
structure went up in the distance. Built largely of Georgia
pine, the main building was two stories high, about 400 feet
long and 150 feet wide. With its many windows, buff-
painted wood, picturesque towers and blue slate roof, it
looked to one writer at *Harper's Weekly* just like "a
latter-day watering place hotel." Its interior, finished in
natural wood, was laid out in a plan very much like that of
the brick building that later replaced it. There were baggage
rooms at ground level and, upstairs, a great inspection hall.
On the surrounding grounds were hospital buildings, doctors' quarters, a bath house, laundry, electric power plant,
kitchens and a dining hall. Some of the old brick-and-stone
buildings dating from the days of the army's fort were
remodeled into dormitory space for detained immigrants,

and some of the navy's now empty magazines, built of heavy masonry, were converted into vaults for storing records. The cost of the whole splendid place, officially opened on January 1, 1892, was about $500,000.

While the new station was being built, the New York State Commissioners of Emigration, resentful that their contract with the Treasury Department had been cancelled in the spring of 1890, refused to allow continued use of Castle Garden. For two years, therefore, immigrants had been crowded into the Barge Office, a stone building with a corrugated-iron annex, in the southeast corner of Battery Park. Named for the barges that once ferried to that landing place from Governor's Island, the Barge Office had been built in 1883 as a depot where all cabin-class passengers could disembark and pass customs inspection. The idea had not worked—steamship companies and the passengers themselves preferred the old, inefficient system of landing at piers scattered up and down both shores of the Hudson. The Barge Office that the Treasury Department had built so proudly, therefore, had scarcely been used when it was turned over to the immigrants in April, 1890. The crowding was far worse, of course, than it had ever been in Castle Garden. Spring and summer were the busiest seasons, and in the ten weeks before the government's fiscal year closed at the end of June, records showed that 118,819 immigrants had been received in these makeshift quarters. In the following twelve months, another 405,665 passed through—nearly 42,000 more than in the previous year. Treasury officials, happy to be in control of their own program, still had to concede that their facilities were "not entirely satisfactory."

The immigrants who came to Ellis Island faced new regulations as well as new buildings. In the spring of 1891, a comprehensive immigration law had been passed, much wider in scope than the old law of 1882. All immigration was now under federal control, and the Superintendent of the new Bureau of Immigration was responsible to the Treasury Department for enforcing a stricter set of rules. In addition to rejecting aliens who fell into the previously established categories of "undesirables," inspectors were to exclude polygamists, people with prison records for crimes involving "moral turpitude," and all "persons suffering from a loathsome or contagious disease." The Contract Labor Law of 1885 was stiffened to keep out immigrants who had even been encouraged to emigrate by American employers' advertisements, and such advertising itself was made illegal. Steamship companies, who were supposed to screen their passengers before leaving Europe, were made responsible for returning deportees to their homelands, and for the cost of their food and lodging while they were in detention here. Aliens who entered the United States illegally, or who became public charges within a year of their arrival (because of some condition existing before they landed), were to be deported. Faced with this formidable task, the new Superintendent of Immigration decided that he needed efficient help at the port of New York, and appointed a Buffalo businessman, Colonel John B. Weber, as the first local commissioner.

Ellis Island had not been in operation for many months before officials began to comment on a change in the immigrants who were arriving. The "old" immigrants from Germany, Ireland, Great Britain and Scandinavia were starting to be outnumbered by "new" immigrants from southern and eastern European nations, such as Italy,

Russia, Poland and Austria-Hungary.

A cholera scare in August, 1892, caused a sharp drop in the number of immigrants, old and new. Strict quarantine was imposed on all ships entering American ports from Europe, and many steamship lines became afraid to transport immigrants. The law of 1891 (with stiffened amendments in 1893) also began to show its effect. A financial panic in 1893, followed by several years of economic depression, discouraged even more immigrants and the number of arrivals continued to drop. The low point was reached in 1898, when Ellis Island's inspectors recorded no more than 178,748 incoming foreigners. Immigration officials in Washington and New York said that the great wave of transatlantic emigration had clearly passed its crest.

It was lucky that the port of New York was not busier at the time. Shortly after midnight on June 14, 1897, a disastrous fire broke out on Ellis Island and the buildings of pine went up in flames as if they had been tinder. A great shower of sparks flew up into the sky as the slate roof of the main building crashed in at one o'clock, and by the morning's early hours there was hardly a trace of the station left. Attracted by the blaze, almost every boat and tug in the harbor rushed to the Island to help guards and doctors save the immigrants who had been sleeping in the hospital and dormitories. There were two hundred people on the Island, but not one life was lost. Most of the patients were safely on the *John G. Carlisle* paddle-wheeler by 1:30, and before dawn they had been taken to Bellevue Hospital. The great irony was that the final contracts for the fine new

Overleaf: The architect's drawing of Ellis Island's second receiving station, this time built of red brick with limestone trim. It opened on December 17, 1900. In the foreground is Island No. 2, site of the general hospital, while Manhattan and the 2 rivers can be seen on the horizon.
(Harper's Weekly, February 26, 1898)

station (cables for telegraph and telephones) had been fulfilled only the day before. Now the work had to begin all over again.

Emergency arrangements had to be made quickly. Several ships carrying large numbers of immigrants sailed into New York Bay on the day after the fire, and inspections were carried out on the piers. Then the doors of the Barge Office opened again. Detained immigrants were squeezed into its annex, and—when there was no more room there—additional quarters for them and space for a small hospital were rented in two large houses on State Street, facing Battery Park. A few months later, better arrangements were made: detainees were housed on an old steamer, the *Narragansett,* docked in the Ellis Island ferry slip, while the sick were farmed out under contract to local hospitals. The small rooms of the Barge Office were hopelessly inadequate for the regular inspections, and the whole building was described in the *New York Tribune* (Dec. 17, 1900) as "grimy, gloomy . . . more suggestive of an inclosure for animals than a receiving station for prospective citizens of the United States." Immigrants who were able to leave the Barge Office without delay faced other problems: they were no longer adequately protected from the swindlers and runners who reappeared in their old haunts near Castle Garden to trap unwary newcomers.

There were difficulties on another level, too. The local Commissioner of Immigration carried on a feud with the head of the bureau in Washington, splitting his politically-appointed staff into fighting factions. Some inspectors succumbed to temptation, and accusations of graft and brutality were made. It was a difficult year for everyone. A serious scandal became public in 1899, and in 1900 hearings held in New York implicated a number of officials. As the number of immigrants rose with returning national prosperity, tensions in the overcrowded Barge Office became almost unbearable. It was time for a fresh start.

Rebuilding of the Ellis Island station pushed ahead as quickly as possible. New structures had been authorized by the government only a few weeks after the fire, and, after a bidding competition open to private architects, the contract had been awarded in August, 1898, to the New York firm of Boring & Tilton. Their building was to be completely fireproof, using nothing but uninflammable materials—floors of concrete, iron railings, beds of iron and wire netting—inside a brick exterior. Their architectural task was not easy, since the facilities they had to design were a combination of railroad station, hospital, prison and hotel. They planned large waiting rooms, dormitories for over a thousand men and women, a restaurant capable of serving thousands of meals a day, hospital wards, docks and wharves, a post office, customs house, telegraph station, offices and staff residences. In between all these facilities, Boring & Tilton managed to preserve some of the small Island's green grass and trees.

The main building, placed on the site of the burned-out wooden one, was built of brick with white limestone trim. Everyone agreed it was an architectural triumph but many writers were uncertain how to describe its appearance—one tried "French Renaissance style . . . accentuated over other types of architecture." The main building, three floors high in the center with two-story wings, was 385 feet long and 165 feet wide. Its four ornamental corner towers reached to a height of 100 feet. Three tall arches spanned the entrance on the west side, while matching arches on the east faced the Hudson River. When it opened at the end of the year, the whole station had cost over $1,000,000—and $500,000 more was needed to complete it.

The station was ready for use, although not quite finished, on December 17, 1900, three and a half years after the fire. On that day, 654 Italians off the *Kaiser Wilhelm II* were the first to enter the new Registry Hall, soon followed by steerage passengers from the *Victoria*, the *Vincenzo Florio* and the *Umbria*. A total of 2,251 immigrants were inspected on opening day.

Only one mistake had been made—and it was a serious one. The architects had believed the immigration officials' estimate that no more than half a million immigrants would ever again arrive in New York in a single year. That proved to be a disastrous miscalculation, and much of Ellis Island's story is one of a frantic struggle for space in which to squeeze the ever-growing numbers of newcomers who flooded into the country during the next fifteen years.

In spite of the fine new buildings built to receive them, immigrants who arrived in the years immediately after Ellis Island's reopening did not get the fair treatment or welcome that the government intended. Some of the employees, particularly those who worked for profit-hungry concessionaires, were often rude and dishonest. Edward Steiner, an immigrant who became a clergyman and teacher, made several transatlantic crossings in order to expose the worst scandals: he recorded that "roughness, cursing, intimidation and a mild form of blackmail" were common on the Island. Employees swore at immigrants as they pushed them around. The restaurant, one of the most profitable concessions, was described by Steiner as "a den of thieves, in which the immigrant was robbed by the proprietor, whose employees stole from him and from the immigrant also." The staple dish was a slice of bread covered with stewed prunes. The bowls, such cutlery as there was, and the floor of the dining room were hardly ever washed. Some immigrants were forced to work at chores in the kitchen. Things were no better at the Money Exchange, where Steiner reported that he was robbed of nearly three-quarters of his money when he changed a European gold piece. In the Registry Hall, inspectors hinted that clearance would come more quickly if they were offered a bribe, and immigrants with large amounts of cash often found themselves "detained." Some inspectors lazily signed blank landing cards, and let unqualified interpreters or even the building's maintenance men pass judgment on the immigrants. Others succumbed to different temptations and quickly admitted pretty girls who agreed to meet them later at a hotel. Once they did receive landing cards, immigrants fell prey to other concessionaires—they were often compelled to buy expensive box lunches even if they did not need them, and the railroad agents sold tickets as profitably as possible (one improbable route to Chicago went through New York State and Virginia).

Steiner's harshest condemnation was for the steamship companies, many of which still practiced "their ancient wrongs upon the most profitable passengers." Steerage on many ships was still a ghastly nightmare, and Steiner advocated its immediate abolition. For one kind of corruption on board, however, the shipping companies could not be blamed: American immigration inspectors who boarded ships in the quarantine area were found to be issuing fake certificates of citizenship, for a fee, and splitting their profits with ships' officers who looked the other way. Immigrants who bought these false papers for five dollars or more were free to land directly on Manhattan. Even then, however, they were not safe: thieves followed groups of the easily recognizable newcomers through the streets, to railroad terminals and even on to the elevated trains, accosted them and often took money from them by force.

It took the President of the United States to clean up this mess. Theodore Roosevelt became President in September, 1901, after William McKinley was assassinated, and he was a man of enormous energy and enthusiasm for reform. During two years as Police Commissioner in New York City he had had practical experience in rooting out corruption, and his reputation for toughness had been established with the famous Rough Riders of the Spanish-American War. Within a month after taking office, Roosevelt began work on the situation at Ellis Island. He replaced the aging local Commissioner of Immigration and his assistant (Thomas Fitchie and Edward McSweeney), as well as the head of the Bureau of Immigration in Washington (Terence Powderly), all of whom were active politicians while in office.

Overleaf: Exhausted and wind-chilled immigrants, bound for the newly reopened station on Ellis Island, huddle together on the small steerage deck of the Red Star liner Westernland out of Antwerp in 1901. Over half of the steerage passengers now arriving at Ellis Island represented the "new" migration from the non-Anglo-Saxon areas of Europe. Original glass slide copyrighted in May, 1902, for the T.H. McAllister Co.
(Museum of the City of New York, Print Archives)

A detained immigrant states his case before a
Board of Special Inquiry in 1897. Corruption was
rampant on Ellis Island at the turn of the
century; inspectors asked for bribes, and immigrants
carrying much cash were often "detained" or
cheated at the Money Exchange.
(Century, February, 1898)

A young Wall Street lawyer, William Williams, was appointed in April, 1902, as the new commissioner. With Roosevelt's backing, Williams earned the antagonism of many influential politicians as he swept Ellis Island clean, awarding (on the basis of merit) new contracts for the food, money and baggage concessions. His only criterion when making these awards was the best service to be offered to immigrants. The new concessionaires were told that they would lose their contracts the moment any dishonesty was spotted. Williams nailed up large signs reminding his employees to treat immigrants with "kindness and consideration," and he imposed penalties for violations of this rule. Employees were no longer allowed to receive favors, such as free passes from the railroads (who naturally wanted to see the greatest possible number of immigrants admitted). Employees were sharply reprimanded for drunkenness, which had once been quite common. One telegraph boy, who gave an immigrant counterfeit coins, was promptly sent to jail on the commissioner's charges. Fines were levied on steamship companies who "forgot" to list certain aliens on their manifests.

Within a few months of this amazing regime, the editors of *Leslie's Weekly* (August 7, 1902) were heaping praise on Mr. Williams—"a thorough, resourceful, and hard-working executive" who had seen to it that "the aliens are now treated in the main quite as considerately as would be crowds of like size and character in the heart of the city." A reporter for *Outlook* (October 4, 1902) wrote that helpless immigrants were treated with "real tenderness." The atmosphere at Ellis Island, thanks to Roosevelt and Williams, had completely changed. The pattern of corruption had been broken, even though perfection in the administration would never be attained. It is a fair judgment, as historian Thomas Pitkin summed up, that Ellis Island was from now on "probably run with as much consideration for the immigrant as its overwhelming problems and the frailty of human nature would permit." Reform had come just in time to meet the pressures of Ellis Island's busiest years, described in the opening chapter of this book.

V
Life and Work in the New World

When an immigrant stepped off the Ellis Island ferry or through the gates of Castle Garden and into the New World, he was not likely to have much spare cash jingling in his pocket (little more than eight dollars, on the average). He had two urgent problems to solve: where to sleep, and how to find a job as quickly as possible. If a relative or a fellow countryman was on hand to meet him, the solutions were easy: the newcomer would be taken home, bedded down in some corner of a small tenement room and introduced the next morning to a sympathetic boss or construction foreman, who was usually an immigrant himself. If a man had no friends in New York, he might find shelter and advice in one of the church-run boarding houses that lined the streets above Battery Park;

The ax and saw were primary tools of the immigrants, starting in the 1600's when colonists cut clearings in the eastern woods. To fell the timber of the Northwest, lumber companies recruited crews like this one, posing in the 1890's. Many lumberjacks were Scandinavian immigrants.
(Courtesy of Weyerhaeuser Company)

or he might wander uptown, asking directions from anyone who spoke his language, until he reached the district where his compatriots were most heavily settled. In the days of the Castle Garden Labor Exchange, hundreds of immigrants found jobs without even setting foot in the city streets, being recruited on the spot to work on distant farms, mines or railroads.

The problems of work and shelter were solved in advance for the many immigrants who landed during much of the nineteenth century with labor contracts already in their pockets. These were the years in which factories and mines sprang up everywhere in the northeastern states, with a new transportation network to link them together. The country faced a serious shortage of cheap, hard-working laborers. American manufacturers advertised in European newspapers, offering to pay the passage of any man willing to work for them. Other industrialists sent their agents across the Atlantic to recruit, for example, teams of expert Welsh and Cornish miners to dig up the coal and iron ore in Pennsylvania. Sometimes all the strong young men of a European village would succumb to the tempting offers of a fast-talking American contractor; they sailed together as a ready-made work crew. Faced with a particularly acute shortage of soldiers and workers during the Civil War, the federal and local governments of the United States did everything possible to encourage this process of mass immigration.

Whether they worked at mining, quarrying, railroading or manufacturing, the immigrant contract laborers were always given America's dirtiest and most dangerous jobs. As the nineteenth-century era of steam and steel began, thousands of Irish farm workers swung picks and shovels to an unfamiliar rhythm as they dug the 350-mile Erie Canal, linking the Great Lakes and the Hudson River, and dozens of smaller waterways throughout the eastern states. Through these canals ran the lifeblood of industrial America—a steady flow of raw materials and manufactured goods. As vital as the task of building them was, it paid the laborers little and was unbelievably hard. One refined Irish visitor to Louisiana in the 1830's was appalled to see gangs of his unlucky countrymen sweating over a canal to link Lake Pontchartrain and New Orleans—"hundreds of fine fellows labouring beneath a sun that at this winter season was insufferably fierce, and amidst a pestilential swamp whose exhalations were fetid to a degree scarcely endurable for a few moments; wading amidst stumps of trees, mid-deep in black mud, clearing the spaces pumped by powerful steam engines; wheeling, digging, hewing, or bearing burdens it made one's shoulders ache to look upon. . . ."

Steam-driven locomotives soon outpaced canal barges, and railroads were built in short webs radiating from every major eastern city. The speed of this construction was frenzied: between 1840 and 1860, some 30,000 miles of track were laid. The Pennsylvania Railroad completed a single-track line between Philadelphia and Pittsburgh in 1854, and railroad building spread to the Midwest in the 1850's—the decade in which construction of a transcontinental line became a political issue. Gangs of immigrant workers—Swedes, Germans and Poles, as well as the Irish—supplied the muscle power to lay this network of iron. When Congress authorized the longest track of all in the 1860's, the Union Pacific line to stretch westward from Nebraska across the prairie, the railroad company offered cheap farmland to immigrants who would sign up to work on this huge project. Hundreds of European men, sustained by the dream of ploughing their own soil, lived for four years in cramped dormitory trains, pushing westward mile by mile to meet the Central Pacific rails advancing from California. Those rails were simultaneously being hammered into place by some fifteen thousand Chinese laborers, or "coolies," who amazed their American coworkers by their strength—and by the fact that they bathed every day. Through mountain ranges, snowstorms, rock slides and a few Indian attacks, these Asiatic immigrants doggedly laid almost three miles of track per day; as many as a thousand of them may have lost their lives as they blasted out tunnels with primitive explosives. At last, on May 10, 1869, the two sets of tracks touched in the Utah wilderness, the last spike (made of gold) was driven, and immigrants from across two oceans drank to the completion of the first American transcontinental railroad. In the following years, some of these men worked on the Northern Pacific, the Southern Pacific and the legendary Santa Fe railways.

Immigrants were passengers, as well as laborers, on the new railroads. During the previous century, Yankee frontiersmen and immigrant farmers had been trekking West— on horseback or on foot, in Conestoga wagons or in the wagon trains of "prairie schooners" that began rolling across the Great Plains in the 1840's. Farmers and land speculators, miners and Mormons, had made the slow, dangerous journey across the continent. But it was the completion of the transcontinental Union Pacific Railroad, combined with the passing of the Homestead Act, that really opened up the central part of the country, the area that Daniel Webster had once dismissed as "a region of savages and wild beasts, of deserts of shifting sands and whirlwinds of dust, of cactus and prairie dogs."

Immigrant farmers now rushed to the area in great numbers, anxious to claim a homestead of 160 acres before the best of the public lands were gone; to gain title, they had only to stay on the land for five years and become American citizens within that time. The railroads, large and small, were anxious to bring in even more settlers who would create passenger and freight traffic for their lines. As part of their construction contracts, they had received from Congress a total of over 180 million acres of land along their rights-of-way, in strips from twenty to one hundred miles wide. Offering this farmland on cheap and easy terms to immigrants, the railroads pasted up posters in European steamship offices, printed multilingual leaflets advertising their area's charms and put into service special "emigrant trains." One enterprising railroad in Nebraska advertised in a Bremen emigrants' newspaper, the *Deutsche Auswanderer Zeitung:* "The Burlington & Missouri River Railroad Company offers for sale millions of acres of the best land in the

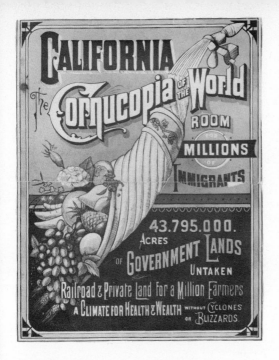

There was room for "millions of immigrants" in California, according to this colored advertising poster. Pamphlets and posters of all kinds, in English and many European languages, were published by railroads and state governments to attract settlers to their regions. *(New York Historical Society, Bella C. Landauer Collection)*

wonderful farming country of Iowa and Nebraska." From its offices in England, this Burlington line sent agents to southern Russia (where they induced colonies of Mennonites to emigrate), to Germany (where Reformed Lutherans responded), to France, Sweden, Norway, Holland, Bohemia and Poland. To cope with the gratifyingly large numbers of farmers arriving each day in Lincoln, Nebraska, the com-

Nebraska's population—swelled by Czechs,
Germans, Swiss and Scandinavians—rose from
30,000 in 1860 to 122,000 10 years later. Some
settlers were given homesteads on the high,
arid plains, where temperatures rose to 110°. On
land fit only for grazing, many

homesteads of only 160 acres could not sustain
farms. The land act of 1904 gave settlers in the driest
regions 640 acres. Photo by
S.D. Butcher, around 1888, near Coburg.

*(Library of Congress, Prints & Photographs
Division)*

pany even erected an Immigrant Home with free cooking facilities and lodgings. Many an immigrant landed at Castle Garden or Ellis Island knowing only one person in America, the Burlington land agent, and only two towns—New York and Lincoln.

The immigrants who settled on homesteads and railroad lands in the prairies and plains did not have an easy reception, generally. Thousands of Norwegians, Swedes and Germans moved into the northern plains, Czechs went to Nebraska, and Russian-German Mennonites to Kansas. There they faced farming conditions they had never seen before. They forced their plows through the matted roots of the prairie grass, searched for water, and looked in vain for wood. They endured dust storms, plagues of grasshoppers, prairie fires and the severest winters ever known in the region. They survived Indian onslaughts—and occasional attacks by cattle ranchers who hated the barbed-wire fences enclosing their formerly free grazing lands. They survived, but often they pined with homesickness for the old country, and they felt desperately lonely—the nearest neighbor might be two miles away and hardly able to communicate in English. Every man had to decide for himself what to plant, when and how. Sometimes it seemed impossible, but they clung to the land, fought it and nurtured it. Occasionally they caught a glimpse of a transcontinental train bearing other immigrants still further west. In 1893, an American historian woke the nation up to the fact that the western frontier, the border where settlements had ended and wildness began, had disappeared. The immigrants had peopled a continent.

When immigrants had been settled in this country for a few years, in the west or on the East Coast, they often came to resent, as American-born workers did, the influx of laborers who followed them from other parts of the Old World. The newest arrivals were always willing to work for low wages, and when jobs were temporarily scarce—as during the depression of 1873—tempers flared. In San Francisco during the late 1870's, Dennis Kearney (a County Cork sailor turned teamster) attracted crowds of unemployed Californians to the empty sand lots where he made

This ingenious family lived in a giant cedar stump near Sedro Woolley, in the forested area of northwestern Washington. When railroads reached that state in the 1880's, its population quadrupled in a decade. Photo by D.R. Kinsey, 1901.
(Library of Congress, Prints & Photographs Division)

inflammatory speeches, ending every harangue with the cry, "The Chinese must go!" Kearney led his rough followers in a series of ugly race riots—running Chinese workers out of factories, burning laundries they owned and threatening employers who hired Chinese laborers. Partly as a result of his political agitation, Chinese residents of San Francisco were temporarily forbidden by local law to own real estate and hold certain jobs. The federal government's Exclusion Act of 1882 banned all further immigration by Chinese laborers. The more than fifty thousand already living in California found it almost impossible to be naturalized as American citizens.

In the East Coast's industrial areas, meanwhile, hundreds of American workingmen found themselves unemployed when their jobs were taken by lower-paid foreigners recruited by their employers in Europe. As methods of mass production were adopted in the old "manufactories" of New England, machines making shoes and textiles took the place of craftsmen, and many a factory owner found it profitable to replace experienced American employees with unskilled but hard-working immigrants. Outraged members of the earliest American trade unions walked out in protest—and found their places taken by still more crowds of immigrants shipped over as strikebreakers. During the Pennsylvania coal miners' strike of 1875, for example, the industrialists brought shiploads of new miners from Europe with bodyguards to protect them. The cause was taken up by the first national precursors of the American Federation of Labor, the Knights of Labor, who successfully urged their 700,000 members to make a political issue of the way in which immigrants were being imported to break strikes and hold down wages. In February, 1885, Congress responded to their appeals and passed the Foran Act or Alien Contract Labor Law, barring American employers from importing immigrants "under contract or agreement to perform labor in the United States, its Territories, and the District of Columbia." The act had the incidental effect of protecting the immigrants themselves, who had often agreed, under the old system, to work for several years at starvation wages before they realized the value of a dollar.

Even after prearranged employment was forbidden, many an immigrant went directly from ship to construction camp or mine. Labor contractors continued to recruit work gangs (and strikebreakers) in the immigrant lodgings of every port. Most men arriving at the turn of the century left their families behind in Europe for a few years. Those who did bring wives and children across the sea were often forced to leave them in the care of city relatives, while they traveled on alone to the rougher but more profitable life of a distant lumber camp, dam or canal project. Wages there sounded attractive—but the disadvantages soon became uncomfortably clear. The work gang's boss or padrone, a middleman of the same nationality as the crew he hired, often turned out to be a parasite rather than an ally of the immigrants. When he arbitrarily lowered wages to increase his personal profit, who was in a position to argue with him? The workers, housed in ramshackle huts or ancient railroad cars, were crowded, uncomfortable and usually dirty. The men often found themselves owing money to the company store where they were forced to buy supplies, or in debt to one another after a night of drinking and card games. It was very hard to save a dollar, and they owed the padrone the cost of their transportation to the camp. They felt the despair of trapped men.

In their bitterness the isolated men sometimes turned against one another. The nation's coal mines, for example, employed several hundred thousand Irishmen, Poles and "Slavs," who fought among themselves as often as they turned in unison against the native American laborers. A miner's life was hard enough to make the most patient man want to strike out in anger. His day began at dawn, when he went down the shaft—but not until the morning whistle blew was he sure that he would work that day, for when the price of coal dropped, the company closed the mine for several days each week. When he did work, a miner's pay was figured by the ton rather than by the hour, so he raced against the clock as he pried chunks of coal from the underground seams and shoveled them into cars. The average miner in 1900 earned about four hundred dollars a year; if his family lived with him, his wife might earn a little by doing laundry or domestic work for the managers, while his children picked out unwanted slate and rock from the heaps of ore. Sons twelve years old or younger lied about their ages so that they could work beside their fathers. The companies wasted little sympathy on their workers. During the 1902 strike of the newly formed United Mine Workers, the president of the Reading Railway (which controlled half the anthracite mines in the country) scoffed at his employees' complaints: "They don't suffer; why, they can't even speak English!"

In other industrial centers, where men worked above ground, the labor was no easier. In the slaughter houses and meat-packing plants of Chicago, the dark steel mills of Youngstown, and the textile factories of Fall River, immigrants toiled for ten or twelve hours each day, six days a week. In the steel industry, an eighty-four-hour week was not uncommon. Rare days of rest like Sundays, Christmas and New Year's Day were often resented more than enjoyed, for when there was no work there was no pay. The average industrial wage around 1900, for both skilled and unskilled workers, was less than ten dollars a week. Rarely could an unskilled laborer earn as much as ten cents per hour. Wages sometimes fell far below subsistence level: in New England's textile mills, inexperienced workers received only $4.50 a week—seventy-five cents for a ten-hour day. These mills, like many other industries, closed down during slow seasons (usually three months of the year), and their employees lived in dread of layoffs, long illnesses and disabling accidents. The rate of industrial accidents was alarmingly high. The most callous employers treated their immigrant workers like cheap machines, to be discarded when broken or worn out. Dangerous and hard as these industrial jobs were, the unskilled immigrants competed fiercely with one another to get them, driving down their own pay scale—for every one hundred dollars earned by a native American, the Italian-born in 1900 earned eighty-four dollars, a Hungarian only sixty-eight dollars and other Europeans as little as fifty-four dollars. Only those native Americans who had been born black worked for lower

Many immigrants spent their lives in mines
digging up the iron ore, coal and copper needed
by industrial America. This Slavic miner,
with an old-fashioned oil lamp in his hat, worked
in the coal fields of Pennsylvania in 1909.
Photo by Lewis Hine.
(George Eastman House)

wages, on the average, than the nation's ten million immigrants. Economists scanned the grim statistics and concluded that 60 per cent of all adult males working in the
United States earned too little to support their families.
Boys and girls of eight or ten did men's work for children's
wages in some factories. They had pale, serious faces and
stooped shoulders. Other sons and daughters moved away
from home (then, at least, there were fewer mouths to
feed) to work as young maids, gardeners or stable boys in
the households of prosperous Americans.

As rapidly as the nation's mills and mines expanded in
the tremendous industrial boom after the Civil War, even
more quickly did its cities grow. In one decade alone,

Italian laborers shovel earth and push boulders out of the path of the Boston-Westchester Railroad. By 1910, when this photograph was taken, immigrants had laid 350,000 miles of railroad track across the continent and paved 200,000 miles of highway. *(Brown Brothers)*

Men from southern Italy prepare to dig up
the street under the Sixth Avenue Elevated
in New York City in 1910. By the 1890's most
immigrants found themselves trapped in cities on
the East Coast, where they might work for
less than $2 a day, building subways and
skyscrapers instead of farming. Photo by Lewis Hine.
*(New York Public Library, Local History &
Genealogy Division)*

1880-1890, the urban population of the United States leaped from fourteen million to twenty-two million. Some of the new city dwellers were unemployed farm workers, gradually forced off the land by the invention of great harvesters, reapers and other labor-saving machines. Greater numbers of the newcomers of the cities were recent immigrants, most of whom had come from European villages and who dreamed of working small farms of their own. As the western frontier filled up with settlers and the price of land rose, these immigrants discovered they were too late, or too poor, to live as they had hoped. By the 1890's hundreds of thousands of them every year found themselves trapped in the already crowded urban centers. A few escaped to livelihoods other than farming—some Portuguese to be fishermen on the East Coast, Poles to grow vegetables in small truck gardens in the suburbs, Italians to cultivate vineyards in the Finger Lakes region or in California. These enterprises required a small hoard of savings. Most immigrants, too poor to move on, remained in the big eastern seaports of New York, Boston, Philadelphia, Baltimore and New Orleans, or moved west no further than the major urban crossroads of the country—Cleveland, Chicago, Cincinnati, Pittsburgh and St. Louis.

The very fact that the immigrants settled in the cities in such unprecedented numbers created a need there for the unskilled manual labor they could provide. Municipalities struggled to pave streets, extend trolley tracks, install new water mains and construct more housing for their residents. Cities expanded at an alarming rate, but still could not cope

Overleaf: Orchard Street, photographed from Hester Street in 1898, was part of the open-air market that filled half a dozen streets on the Lower East Side. Only Bombay had a denser population, and it is said that as many as 4,000 immigrants lived on 1 block. Photo by Joseph Byron.
(Museum of the City of New York, Byron Collection)

133

with the new demands. Traffic jams of horse-drawn vehicles snarled downtown streets, tenements began to encroach on once elegant shopping districts and makeshift huts spread out along some river banks as the newcomers searched for room to live.

Increasing numbers of immigrants simply stayed in the port where they had disembarked and New York City—on the doorstep of Ellis Island—suffered the worst growing pains of all. Its population had passed one million in 1875, and by 1900 it was trying to find space for 3.5 million residents—1.3 million of them, or 37 per cent, were foreign-born. Thousands of immigrant men found work in the city's construction crews, laboring as ditch-diggers, hod-carriers and stone-cutters. As long as they had strong arms, it did not matter if they could not speak English, read or operate a complex machine. They graded road beds, laid paving blocks and buried gas pipes. They dug the first Interborough Rapid Transit subway tunnels, laid cables for Broadway's novel electric lights and telephones, spanned the East River with bridges and raised the famous Flatiron Building twenty stories into the sky. Unfortunately, in all this construction activity, the building of new housing lagged far behind (no government funds were allotted for housing until World War I).

The slums in which most of New York's immigrants lived were infamous—though not much worse than those of Chicago or Boston. A housing law of 1879 had banned windowless rooms and by 1900, reformer Jacob Riis believed, the very worst of the city's old buildings (dating back to before the Civil War) had been demolished. Nevertheless, the New York State Tenement House Commission that year reported that over a third of Manhattan's residents were crowded into forty-three thousand tenement houses which were dark, stuffy, dirty and hopeless as places in which to raise a normal family. Each floor in one of these buildings might have fourteen rooms, many of which—particularly in the "dumbbell"-shaped tenements—received their only light and ventilation from dark air shafts. Often a family with four or five children managed to live in one small room, while those with a little more space

Many immigrant men, who left their wives
in Europe for the first few years, earned less
than $10 a week and could not afford to set up
households of their own. They boarded with tenement
families anxious to earn an extra dollar, or
stayed in lodgings like this Slavic establishment
in a factory district near New York City,
photographed in 1912 by Lewis Hine.
*(New York Public Library, Local History
& Genealogy Division)*

would allow a paying boarder to sleep in a corner. Pools of
stagnant water filled the unlit cellars. Behind some buildings a row of privies stood in the yard. The alleys between
the tenements, littered with filth and garbage, were here
and there so narrow that neighbors in adjoining buildings
could reach out and shake hands from their windows. Rats
scampered everywhere, and the situation was not improved
when a rustic tenant occasionally tried keeping chickens or
a goat to live off the garbage. The stench, indoors and out,
was terrible in the summer. Disease spread almost as

quickly as the frequent fires: nearly 40 per cent of the slum dwellers suffered from tuberculosis, and in one district of tenements six out of every ten babies died before their first birthday.

The crowding did give the immigrants the comfort of familiar language and customs, for they clustered together in groups according to the country, province or even village from which they had come. By 1910, most large cities in the United States had a well-defined "Little Italy," "Little Poland," a Jewish "ghetto" and perhaps a "Chinatown." But the companionship of their countrymen could do little to ease the immigrants' pain at living in such a place. The dirt and smell, the sickness and poverty—these were enough to make any man feel that the dream of America had turned into a nightmare. His lack of industrial skills or English could trap the most intelligent man into manual labor for life; his wages were so close to the cost of living that it took superhuman efforts to save enough for escape. One Italian army officer, for example, a man of important social rank at home, emigrated when he resigned from the service, but in New York the only work he could find was hard manual labor in a piano factory. He earned eleven dollars a week, barely enough to keep his family alive, and there were many times when they had no food in the house. When construction workers finished a project, they found themselves back where they started—looking for a job, with few savings. This time, though, they were a little older and weaker; with every project they risked injuries that might make them unfit for any work.

Some immigrants had the skill to work with their hands in other ways. They included almost two out of every three Russian and Polish Jews who were pouring into New York's Lower East Side at the turn of the century (in some parts of Europe they had been forbidden to own farmland, and had been forced to learn urban trades). In overwhelming numbers, these Jewish immigrants went into the city's "needle trades," making clothes of all sorts, furs and hats for men and women. Because there were so many immigrants competing for this work, and because the garment manufacturers strained to undercut one another's prices,

An immigrant family works at home,
sewing men's clothing. Children as young as 7,
who could thread needles and pull basting stitches,
worked before school and again in the
evenings, adding 50¢ or $1 to
the weekly income. Photo by Hiram Myers.
(New York Public Library, Picture Collection)

the clothing workers fared worse than the laborers in
factories and mines. Paid at piecework rates, they rarely
earned more than two hundred dollars a year, and they
worked extraordinarily long hours. In 1895, when thousands of them went on strike to demand a ten-hour day (7
A.M. to 6 P.M., with one hour off for dinner), they got
nowhere; two years later, some girls were reported to be
working a 108-hour week. In many of New York's clothing
factories, girls outnumbered men; but employees of both
sexes had to put in a minimum of thirteen hours a day
(eighty hours per week) to earn a maximum of six dollars—
sometimes as little as three dollars. David Dubinsky, later to
become president of the I.L.G.W.U. in 1911 earned three
dollars a week at his first job as a cloak-cutter. The

A mother tries to make a home in a cramped rear room in one of New York's tenements, around 1908. These rooms, stifling in summer, were heated in winter only by the tenant's coal stove. Many sent their children to scavenge for lumps of fuel in the New York Central freight yards. Photo by Lewis Hine. *(George Eastman House)*

employer even had ways of reducing the pay—girls were fined twenty-five cents for giggling, fifty cents for staring out of the window, and in some shops they had to pay for the thread in their sewing machines and "rent" the hooks on which they hung their larger flowery hats. If they were bold enough to complain to factory inspectors about dirt and dangers that violated city laws, the inspector might do no more than report their complaints to the boss—and the grumblers promptly lost their jobs. The hazardous conditions under which they sometimes worked attracted national attention in March, 1911, when a disastrous fire swept through the Triangle Waist Company one afternoon and killed about 145 employees, most of them young women. The ten-story building, in which the company rented the top three floors, was technically fireproof. But the blaze—fanned by draughts from open windows, and spreading quickly on the flammable laces and flimsy fabrics being sewn into summer "shirtwaists"—gutted the garment factory's quarters. Access to the single fire escape was blocked, and many of the victims died when they leaped from window ledges in panic, their hair and clothes in flames, onto the mounting pile of bodies on the sidewalk below. The fire brigade's ladders reached only to the seventh floor, and their nets were not strong enough to catch people jumping from that height. Every available ambulance in Manhattan was needed to carry away the dead.

The tenements of New York did not often make the headlines, but their scale of disaster was equally horrifying: comprising less than a third of Manhattan's buildings, they had more than half of its fires. In many of these smaller firetraps were women, men and children who spent their days sewing under conditions worse than those in the most disreputable garment shop. Under the so-called sweating system, these workers were supplied with materials by a contractor who paid for each piece of work completed and returned. When the rate of payment was driven down by the grasping middleman who farmed out the sewing, the work was sometimes accelerated to a desperate pace. More often, the task was prolonged to fifteen or eighteen hours a day. Many of the immigrants who accepted this work were women with small babies, invalids or old people who could not find factory jobs, or children too young to be legally employed. Usually they worked in their own room, seated at the single window or straining their eyes by the oil lamp on the table. But sometimes the whole floor of a tenement would be occupied by a "sweatshop." This usually evaded the city's requirements for a license, and several men and women would work there all day and half the night, without enough light, air, sanitation or safety precautions. Grateful for the work, they were too poor to care.

Sewing for the garment makers was not the only kind of work that could be done in the home. There were artificial flowers to be made—one cent for every seven paper roses— or nut meats to be shelled by the thousand. Mothers and daughters of many nationalities spent their days making lace, garters and paper boxes, or pasting linen onto the tin covers of pocket flasks. German and Bohemian families were particularly adept at rolling cigars, and their children as small as three years old were taught how to straighten the tobacco leaves.

The children of all impoverished immigrants were expected to help with the family's income, even when both parents went out to work. To free the mother for her factory job or sewing tasks, one of the daughters would mind the baby. Young sons acted as assistant lamplighters, going out at 4 A.M. to extinguish the gas streetlights before breakfast and school. Older boys found dozens of odd jobs to do late into the evening—running errands, delivering telegrams, shining shoes, selling newspapers or hawking baskets of flypaper and matches through the streets.

The work and poverty were hard to endure, but nothing new for many of the immigrants, who had known back home what it felt like to go hungry or to sweat in the fields until they ached all over. The sufferings that were the hardest to bear were the new, inner pains that seemed to have no name. The immigrants have been called "the uprooted," "the children of loneliness," and modern psychologists would say more prosaically that they suffered from "alienation." They lived in a world where they felt they did not belong. They knew that they were strangers in America, and even if they prospered here, a sense of loss pervaded their lives. Part of them always remained in the Old World.

In the small villages from which most of the immigrants had come, they had tilled the soil in the tradition of their grandfathers. The old ways were best, they said, and changes came slowly. Within the small world of fields, church, manor house and inn, every villager was connected to his neighbors by lines of marriage, legal obligations, mutual protection and respect. The only strangers were pilgrims, peddlers or gypsies. No matter how poor a man was, or how small his plot of land, he had a sense of dignity. To be driven off that land and away from his village was a total calamity for the peasant, robbing him of his livelihood, his self-respect and place in life. To be paid to do casual labor for other men was degrading.

In the cities of the New World, the immigrant too often found that degradation permanent. Trapped in a landscape of brick and steel where he could hardly see the sky, he worked at tasks not fitting for a man used to sowing and reaping: he dug endless ditches for strange uses, or hammered out dismembered parts of objects on an assembly line. Here a man was not hired for a year or season, as in the Old Country, but for a day or even an hour. Distasteful as the new labor was, he never knew when it would be abruptly taken away from him.

Since a man had to work when he could, he had little time to celebrate the saints' days and happy festivals that had once given meaning to his year. The work in sweatshop and factory did not vary with the seasons, and one day seemed no different from the rest. Some men worked seven days a week, in fact, and did not even observe a day of rest at Easter. When a national festival was celebrated in church on Sunday, it somehow did not feel the same. The priest or rabbi might have come from a strange province, the ritual sounded unfamiliar on his tongue and the church itself was sometimes nothing more than a converted store or tenement room. Here was no bell to summon everyone within hearing, no graveyard filled with departed friends—who knew where the dead were buried in the city? In smaller towns, where few of their countrymen had yet settled, immigrants might have trouble finding a church to go to. Roman Catholics from Austria, Poland or Italy, for example, barely recognized the Irish-dominated churches as belonging to their own faith. Immigrants of the Lutheran and Eastern Orthodox churches split into small national factions in this country, while ten Jewish men tended to form a synagogue because they had emigrated from the same town. In the New World, God Himself sometimes seemed dangerously distant.

The men who worshipped with him and worked beside him often seemed strange to the new immigrant, even if they did speak his own language. They no longer touched their caps respectfully to their bosses or other superiors—in fact, they sometimes behaved as if they had no superiors, as if every man was as good as the next. They read newspapers, listened to the opinions of the ward boss, voted in elections after they had become citizens and argued about affairs that were not the business of a humble man. The European peasant believed that a man should keep to his own station in life. He regretted that in the new city the most presumptuous men—who were boastful and ambitious—seemed to prosper the soonest. He saw that the men who did not succeed often abandoned their old standards in even worse ways—they gambled obsessively, hoping to trick fortune for the rewards they found hard to earn by working, or they wasted money on liquor. Some went hat in hand to beg for charity, while others found it easier to get what they wanted by theft and murder. A few escaped from the pressures around them by withdrawing into a world of shadows and nightmares: they knew that hostile strangers whispered about them, they said, and they heard heavy footsteps following them home at night. Mental illness, gambling, alcoholism, despair and crime were the specters that haunted the slums.

A man might evade them all, but it was not as easy to escape from a more common affliction—loneliness. At the turn of the century, male immigrants from some countries outnumbered their women by seven or eight to one, and they worked here alone for five years or more before they had the money to send for their wives and children. When time for the reunion came, the man might go down to Battery Park dressed in a secondhand American suit, perhaps wearing his prize possession—an American straw hat. As the crowds of immigrants poured off the Ellis Island ferry, he strained to catch sight of his wife and was momentarily startled to see her in the kerchief and peasant skirts of the old country. Looking exhausted and older than he had remembered, she did not recognize him at first, and his children, so big that they were strangers, stared at him curiously. The man knew that he was well on his way to becoming an American; he had not realized that his wife, fresh from the village where nothing ever changed, was not only five years behind him—but a century. Taking his family home on the elevated train, he was embarrassed at the way she cringed at the noise, while his children shrieked at the tall buildings and the other passengers smiled in amusement at the "greenhorns."

When they reached the tenement that was home, the wife looked with horror at the dark, airless room. Was this the way her husband lived in America, where the streets were paved with gold and any man might make a fortune? Used to sweeping out a small cottage whose doors opened onto a garden, and spreading laundry out in the sun to bleach and dry, the peasant woman did not know how to cope with housecleaning in a tenement. Here everything seemed dirtier—ashes from the coal-burning stove settled on every surface, and the smoke from the cheap kerosene in the oil lamp blackened the ceiling. Old wallpaper peeled off in patches. In many buildings a communal faucet or pump on the landing was the only source of running water, which had to be heated on the stove. With little money to spare for soap and brushes, it was hard to make much of an impression on the room, harder still to keep the children clean. Disposing of garbage was another new problem: in the village little had gone to waste, for food did not spoil in the cool cellars and pantries there, and the pig or goat ate whatever scraps were flung out of the kitchen door. Too tired to walk down flights of stairs to containers in the back

A street market in New York City, 1906.

(Library of Congress, Prints & Photographs Division)

alley, some women got rid of their rubbish in the simplest way—by throwing it out of the tenement window.

On the streets outside, other problems waited. In the first place, the crowds were terrifying—four thousand people might live in one block of the Lower East Side. Before the voyage, the peasant woman had never seen any place busier than the market square where she occasionally traded surplus produce for staples such as salt; she had provided all the food her family ate from her own vegetable garden and farmyard. Now she had to buy every meal for cash. She made her way to the marketplace on the Lower East Side—Canal and Hester streets, crossed by Orchard, Ludlow, Essex, Norfolk and Suffolk—where unbelievable numbers of men and women shouted at each other in a dozen languages, as they jostled their way around pushcarts piled with merchandise. Just to find what she wanted was a problem. There were piles of fish, meats, chickens, ripe cheeses, fruit, pickles and huge loaves of black bread. Interspersed between the food stalls were other carts laden with glasses and tinware, remnants of lace and carpeting, boots, stockings for six cents a pair and children's underwear for a nickel. The pushcart vendors bawled out their wares and prices in a strange mixture of Yiddish, German, Russian and English phrases; back on the sidewalk were shopkeepers competing for business, while through the center of the street wandered peddlers selling suspenders, scarves or bagels. The immigrant woman had to face this ordeal every day, and she had to be constantly on her guard, for the vendors might speak in the old language but they did not deal in the old ways—food was often spoiled or too expensive. Friday mornings seemed worst of all, for on that day the Jewish housewives were all out early to buy supplies for the Sabbath.

A few immigrant women found the marketing and other problems of life in a large American slum too much to cope with. "She loved quiet, and hated noise and confusion," one resident of New York's Little Italy wrote about his mother. "Here she never left the house unless she had to. She spent her days, and the waking hours of the nights, sitting at that one outside window staring up at the little patch of sky above the tenements. She was never happy here and, though she tried, could not adjust herself to the poverty and despair in which we had to live.... At the end of three years my mother, who had become ill, went back to Italy. When she could no longer write us, others wrote for her.... She lived only one year after returning to Sulmona."

The thought of giving up and going home tempted many immigrants, and every year hundreds of them did sail back across the Atlantic. The wife who spent her days in a dark room, stitching endless seams or twisting paper into petals, filled her mind with pleasant memories of her sunny birthplace; she forgot the reasons for their emigration. In the evenings she pestered her husband: "Let's go back. We were happier there." "What would we live on? We sold the land. How can we pay for the crossing?" Letters from home caused more argument: accounts of weddings or christenings brought tears of homesickness to the woman's eyes, while relatives' requests for a little money made the man furious. Unable to face the recurring quarrels, the fear of seeing his family go hungry or the occasional shame of living with a wife who earned more than he could, a man might find it easier to leave home. Some husbands simply vanished, but so many marriages were formally broken that by 1903 the Lower East Side had the highest divorce rate of any district in New York.

But most immigrant families clung together, found strength in each other, and struggled for years to make the promise of America come true. With a combination of much work and a little luck, they overcame all the odds against them. As the years went by, trade unions like the I.L.G.W.U. saw that working conditions were improved and wages raised to a reasonable level, so that it became possible to save a little. In a modest way the immigrants prospered, often opening their own small businesses and serving their neighbors as shopkeepers, bakers, undertakers and barbers. Italians opened fruit stores and bootblacking parlors, Jewish immigrants hung out signs that said "Tailor," and the Chinese started laundries in all parts of the city. Some immigrants saved enough to buy houses of their own in working-class districts on the city's fringes, at the far ends of the subway line. They became American citizens. When their children graduated from public school and earned good wages, success came all the more easily to the family.

The children were the immigrants' greatest source of pride—and anxiety. They embodied the painful transition from the Old World to the New, and the fact that they were "little Americans" caused many strains in the family relationships. They went to public schools for five hours a day, where they learned to read and write. Seated at the lamp-lit table at home in the evening, an Italian or Russian-Jewish father might learn from his own small children the ABC's, as well as his first words of English. His heart was filled with pride and hope for the future—he wanted his sons to learn more than he knew, to be better men than he could be. But the children, sensing their advantage, soon questioned their father's authority in all matters. They would contradict him ("But at school the teacher says . . ."), and sometimes they dared to disobey him. Learning American customs, they sometimes voiced their shame or contempt for the old way of doing things, and then the parents would shake their heads in sadness and anger. Was it right that a son should spend his free time out on the street, or that a growing girl should giggle in the hallway with a boy and no chaperone? The best of daughters came home with strange ideas: she wanted to do gymnastics at school, or, as she grew up, to play an active role in the synagogue or work outside the home, perhaps on equal terms with men in a shop. Sons and daughters were unanimous in refusing to marry suitable partners chosen by their parents. They would marry for love, they announced—and so many of them abandoned the old way of finding a spouse that the Jewish *shadchen* or marriage broker had to supplement his income by writing letters, making translations and teaching Hebrew and English. Some Jewish parents could adjust to the idea of romance, but they were beyond consolation when their sons, working their way up in the Gentile business world, spent Saturdays in the office and said they were not free to come home on holy days in mid-week.

Understandably, then, anxious parents were often deep-

Immigrant children salute the flag in the
Mott Street Industrial School, around 1889.
Because so many mothers left home at dawn for
work, the teachers' job included reminding
youngsters to comb their hair and wash
their faces. Photo by Jacob Riis.
*(Museum of the City of New York, Jacob A. Riis
Collection)*

ly suspicious of the places where children might learn alien ways. Some Roman Catholic mothers warned their offspring to stay away from the Henry Street Settlement or Hull House, because—attractive as the recreation there might be—they were part of a plot to convert unwary youngsters to Protestantism. One Italian remembers being so terrified by these rumors that he did not dare drink from the Woman's Christian Temperance Union water fountain in front of his neighborhood settlement house. But the well-meaning men and women who worked in these social welfare institutions and in the city's schools, playgrounds and libraries were the agents of no sinister movement— simply of America herself. In the parks and settlement houses, the immigrants' children learned American games and songs and the ways in which friendly people with different backgrounds could adapt to live with each other. In school they saluted the flag, rattled off the names and dates of American history and celebrated national holidays by reciting patriotic poems. When the schools closed at three o'clock, hundreds of children went directly to the local branch of the New York Public Library where they did their homework and clamored around the librarian, asking for help in selecting new books in English. Favorites among the Jewish children of the Lower East Side were *Uncle Tom's Cabin* and volumes of Bible stories. From the Chatham Square branch alone, by 1903, immigrant children were taking home a thousand English books each day. When they outgrew public schools and local libraries, many of these enthusiastic learners went to free evening classes at the Educational Alliance. At the Cooper Union it cost nothing to study engineering and art, to use the reading room or museum, or to go to the popular Sunday evening lectures. On summer evenings there were concerts in Lewisohn Stadium. An immigrant's son with little money but enough brains could even get a university education at City College. Given the chance, it seemed as if these voracious youngsters had the energy to see, hear and learn everything under the American sun.

The new knowledge did not flow in only one direction, for native Americans had much to learn, in turn, from the immigrants. In New York, the Jewish press, theaters and coffee houses added zest to the city's cultural life. In the hands of immigrant editors and publishers—Carl Schurz, Joseph Pulitzer, Abraham Cahan, Joseph Keppler and Edward Bok—newspapers and magazines like the St. Louis *Post-Dispatch*, the New York *World*, the *Jewish Daily Forward, Puck* and the *Ladies' Home Journal* introduced new political and social ideas to nationwide audiences. The humblest immigrants were more innovative than they realized: banding together into mutual-aid societies like the Jewish *verein* (societies) and *landsmanshaften*, the Lithuanian Benevolent Society and the Polish National Alliance, they gave their members burial funds, sick benefits and free loans when needed, in return for dues as low as twenty-five cents a month (some Greek societies taxed members one cent for each loaf of bread they ate). Decades later, these programs became familiar to all Americans in the forms of life, unemployment and medical insurance, social security and community chests. More good ideas crossed the Atlantic than can easily be counted. The German immigrants introduced kindergartens and the idea of the state-endowed university; they brought with them their Sunday band concerts and Christmas celebrations, they founded symphony orchestras in nearly every large city of the United States, and they turned their singing societies into American glee clubs. Their *turnverein* and the Czech *sokol* (gymnastic and social societies) laid the groundwork for the Y.M.C.A. Scandinavians introduced home economics and manual-training courses into the public schools, and founded the agricultural 4-H clubs. The Italians brought the opera.

Every one of the millions of immigrants who came to this country built a tiny part of America, each in his own way. As Professor Oscar Handlin wrote, "Once I thought to write a history of the immigrants in America. Then I discovered that the immigrants *were* American history."

Some of the newcomers made such an unusual personal contribution that their faces stand out from the huge crowd. Many of them—like the famous Americans whose portraits are shown on these pages—sailed in steerage and passed through Castle Garden or Ellis Island. Others—such as America's first saint, Mother Frances Xavier Cabrini from Italy, the Dutch writer Hendrik Willem Van Loon, and the Russian-born inventor of the helicopter, Igor Sikorsky—had the means to travel in the cabin classes and be inspected on board their ships. Some immigrants bypassed New York completely, landing in Philadelphia, Boston, Montreal and other ports: their numbers include Hungarian-born journalist Joseph Pulitzer, David Sarnoff of R.C.A. and microbiologist Dr. Selman Waksman, both immigrants from Russia, and Alexander Graham Bell, who came across the border from Canada.

Many of the famous immigrants arrived in the years before there were landing stations to receive them. John Peter Zenger, a German-born printer who fought for freedom of the press; Haym Salomon, the patriotic Polish Jew who helped finance the Revolution; John J. Astor, German-born trader and philanthropist; chemist Eleuthere du Pont de Nemours from France; the black poet Phillis Wheatley, who came as a slave-child from Senegal—these and many others arrived in this country in the eighteenth century. In the early nineteenth century, before Castle Garden became a depot, came John James Audubon, the French ornithologist; the first woman doctor, Elizabeth Blackwell, from England; John Ericsson, Swedish steamship builder; Carl Schurz, German-born political reformer; naturalist John Muir and steel millionaire and philanthropist Andrew Carnegie, both from Scotland; sculptor Augustus Saint-Gaudens from Ireland; the Swiss zoologist Louis Agassiz—and many dozens of others who achieved fame in the later 1800's. By far the greatest number of prominent immigrants came during the great wave of "intellectual" migration from European countries that fell under totalitarian regimes just before and after World War II. Led, perhaps, by physicist Albert Einstein from Germany and Russian-born composer Igor Stravinsky, the number of internationally famous scientists, psychologists, artists, writers and musicians who became American citizens in the 1930's and 1940's can be counted literally in the hundreds.

The immigrants who passed through Castle Garden and

Ellis Island, between 1855 and the 1920's, arrived as steerage passengers. Because they were all too familiar with poverty and hard work, several of them became famous in this country for fighting to improve the lot of their fellow laborers. Samuel Gompers, who became first president of the American Federation of Labor, was born in London to poor Dutch-Jewish parents and began work there as a cigar-maker when he was only ten. With his parents and five brothers and sisters, he arrived at Castle Garden on July 30, 1863, and rose through union ranks before serving as the A.F.L.'s leader for nearly forty years. Another union leader, Philip Murray of the United Steel Workers of America and the C.I.O., was a sixteen-year-old coal miner from Scotland when he arrived at Ellis Island on Christmas Day, 1902. One of America's leading social reformers, journalist Jacob Riis, was the son of a Danish school teacher. Running away from an unhappy love affair, he passed through Castle Garden in the summer of 1870. From firsthand experience, he wrote about life in the New World's slums and factories, and his crusading work as journalist, lecturer and photographer probably saved many lives. Other immigrants turned to politics as the means of improving life and work in their adopted country.

"The most interesting radical ever to pass, eastbound or westbound, through the gates of Ellis Island," in the opinion of one commissioner there, was Emma Goldman. When she entered the United States in 1886, she was just a seventeen-year-old Russian Jewish girl who did not stand out in the crowd of immigrants in Castle Garden. But a few years later her name was in every newspaper in the country. Working in a clothing factory in Rochester, she joined the anarchist political movement when she was twenty, and in 1893 she was imprisoned for inciting a riot. She became the lifelong friend and coworker of Alexander Berkman, a Lithuanian-born anarchist and editor of a political paper, *Mother Earth*. Emma's fiery speeches attracted wide attention.

In 1916 Emma Goldman was sent to prison again for advocating birth control, and in 1917, for obstructing the military draft. She was detained on Ellis Island with

Emma Goldman (1869-1940), anarchist,
deported from Ellis Island for her political opinions
in 1919. She was 17 when she emigrated
from Russia, passing through Castle Garden in 1886.
*(Courtesy of National Park Service, Augustus F.
Sherman Collection)*

Berkman and hundreds of other political prisoners during the days of the "Red Scare," and deported on December 21, 1919, on the *Buford*—a military transport ship that carried 249 deportees to Russia by way of Finland.

Emma left Russia in 1921, disillusioned with Lenin's dictatorship; she returned to the United States as a visitor on a lecture tour, took an active part in the Spanish Civil War and died in Toronto in 1940.

It was more usual for radicals whose political ideas were unacceptable in Europe to find refuge in America, rather than to be deported from here. Because he was an active member of a students' Socialist club, opposing the regime of the "Iron Chancellor" Bismarck, Charles Steinmetz was forced to flee from Germany in the middle of the night. He escaped imprisonment, but he also missed receiving his Ph.D. in mathematics from the University of Breslau. He continued studying in Switzerland, barely making ends meet by tutoring and writing, until his roommate, Oscar Asmussen, persuaded him to emigrate to America with him. They sailed together in the steerage of the *Champagne* and appeared at Castle Garden on June 3, 1889. The inspectors were appalled at the sight of the strange young man whose name was Karl August Rudolf Steinmetz: he was a hunchback, barely over four feet tall in spite of his twenty-four years, and he was exhausted from the journey and the effects of a bad cold. He mumbled answers to their questions in German, and when asked if he knew any English, he answered, "A few." Years later, Steinmetz remembered how hopeless he had looked: "When I landed at Castle Garden, from the steerage of a French liner, I had ten dollars and no job, and could speak no English." The inspectors ordered him to the detention pen to be deported. Only the quick lies of Asmussen, who asserted that his own money really belonged to this "wealthy and eccentric scientist," obtained his release.

Asmussen's words were prophetic: Steinmetz certainly was eccentric, and his fame as a scientific genius was to make him rich. Steinmetz began work for twelve dollars a week in the engineering plant of a fellow German in Yonkers. Three years later he stunned the audience at a meeting of the American Institute of Electrical Engineers when—perched up on a chair to read his paper—he announced his discovery of the Law of Hysteresis, explaining the influence of magnetism on electrical motors. Steinmetz moved to the General Electric Company in 1893, when the big firm bought out his former employer, and became known to the nation as "the Wizard of G.E." The company valued his genius so highly that it built him a laboratory in his Victorian house in Schenectady—which the eccentric inventor shared with an astonishing array of orchids and strange pets, including a gila monster, crows, alligators and a monkey named Jenny. Steinmetz proved that electricity could be transmitted over long distances if alternating current, not direct current, was used. He invented lightning arrestors to protect electrical systems from storm damage. And in 1922 he astounded the world when he became the first man to create lightning in his laboratory: "Modern

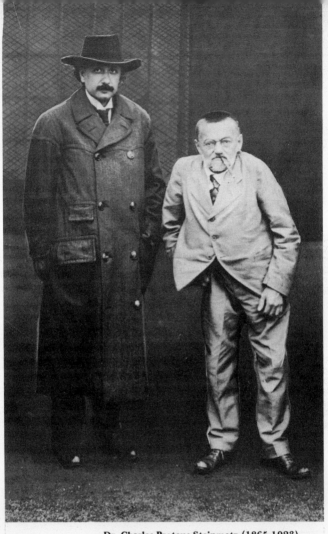

**Dr. Charles Proteus Steinmetz (1865-1923),
electrical engineer, mathematician and inventor,
photographed with another world-famous
immigrant from Germany, Albert Einstein.
Steinmetz came through Castle Garden in 1889.**
*(Courtesy of General Electric Company,
Schenectady)*

Irving Berlin (born 1888), songwriter,
at his piano in August, 1948. His father, a
Russian rabbi named Baline, is said to have led
his family of 8 children through
the first station on Ellis Island in 1893.
*(Library of Congress, Prints & Photographs
Division)*

Jove Hurls Thunderbolts at Will," the newspapers reported. During his thirty years at G.E., Steinmetz patented over two hundred inventions, and his name was ranked with those of Edison, Marconi and Bell. His name was linked, too, with that of another immigrant, Dr. Michael Pupin of Columbia University, an outstanding physicist and inventor who was originally a Serbian shepherd boy. Pupin arrived at Castle Garden in 1874, aged fifteen, alone.

Americans may not always recognize the names of scientists like Steinmetz, but everyone knows the songs of Irving Berlin, another immigrant. The flames of a Russian *pogrom* in 1892 burned down the house in which Israel Baline was born, in Temun, Siberia. Although he was only four years old at the time, he has never forgotten that terrifying night, when he lay on a blanket beside the road and watched the fires blazing in the darkness; next morning, the village was a pile of ashes. Rabbi Baline, his father, fled from the persecution, bringing Israel and his seven other children to the United States in 1893. They sailed in steerage, bringing with them frying pans and a huge feather mattress. During the crossing, an open penknife fell on young Israel from the bunk overhead, scarring him on the forehead for life.

The New World was kinder. Growing up on New York's Lower East Side, Israel Baline worked as a newsboy and singing waiter, until his talent for writing song lyrics earned him a job with a music publisher in 1909. Under the name of Irving Berlin, he became world-famous as the composer of over one thousand popular songs, including *Alexander's Ragtime Band* (1911), the nostalgic *White Christmas* (was he dreaming of the snows of Siberia?), *Always* and *God Bless America*. For *Miss Liberty* in 1949 he set to music the words of Emma Lazarus' poem, "Give me your tired, your poor . . ." Broadway musicals for which he has written scores include *Annie Get Your Gun* (1946) and *Call Me Madam* (1950). Irving Berlin is said to have earned more money from his work than any other writer of music in history.

Another almost legendary immigrant, Knute Rockne, arrived in American the same year as Irving Berlin. Rockne's father, a carriage-maker from the Norwegian mountain village of Voss, traveled to the Chicago World's Fair of 1893 to exhibit his prize-winning vehicles. Liking what he saw of this country, he sent for his family. Mrs. Rockne, a prudent woman who tied her three daughters and small son together with long ribbons as they disembarked, landed in New York before the fair was over, probably passing through the first station on Ellis Island in the late summer of 1893. In Chicago, they went almost at once to the exposition, where five-year-old Knute got lost overnight among the glittering white palaces filled with amazing crowds, popcorn, pink lemonade and real Indians. The Rocknes moved into the rough neighborhood of Logan Square, settled by recent Irish and Swedish immigrants, and Knute grew up playing primitive and usually violent football on the streets. His nose was flattened by a baseball bat.

After leaving public school, Knute worked in the Post Office until, at twenty-two, he had saved enough money to enter the University of Notre Dame. Four years older than his classmates, he worked very hard and became the college's best chemistry student and captain of its football team. All sport fans known the subsequent story of Notre Dame's amazing victory over Army in 1913: the unknown players from Indiana defeated the "unbeatable" team largely with the forward passes perfected by Rockne, who with this technique changed football from a game of force into one of speed and skill. Rockne became Notre Dame's football coach (and chemistry instructor), training more All-American players than any other coach of his day. Most famous of his players were the "Four Horsemen" of 1924. A perfectionist who insisted on fair play, Knute Rockne revolutionized American football and taught a generation of younger coaches. When he was killed in a 1931 plane crash outside Kansas City, millions of Americans mourned the death of the forty-three-year-old immigrant whose name was already a legend.

Like Rockne's father, another enthusiastic visitor to the Chicago World's Fair in 1893 was Leopold Frankfurter, a Viennese merchant descended from a long line of rabbis. Early the next year he sent for his wife Emma, his four sons and two daughters, who sailed from Hamburg in the steerage of a typical immigrant ship called the *Marsala*, passing through Ellis Island on August 10, 1894. The Frankfurters settled in a German neighborhood on the Lower East Side of New York, where eleven-year-old Felix Frankfurter went to P.S. Twenty-five, then to the City College of New York, where an immigrant's son could get a good free education. In every spare moment, he read newspapers and books in the New York Public Library and at Cooper Union. He graduated from C.C.N.Y. third in his class when he was nineteen, and was later first in his class at Harvard Law School. He worked as a lawyer in Washington for a few years, then joined the faculty of the Harvard Law School in 1919. He became an adviser and close friend of Franklin Roosevelt, and in 1939 the President named him

Knute Rockne (1888-1931), football coach
of the University of Notre Dame. His family
emigrated from their Norwegian village when
he was 5, probably passing through Ellis Island
in the summer of 1893. Photo by H.C. Elmore.
*(Courtesy of University of Notre Dame,
Department of Sports Information)*

to the Supreme Court, where Frankfurter gave twenty-three
years of his life to public service in the liberal tradition.

Edward Joseph Flanagan, a farm manager's son from
Roscommon, Ireland, was a tall, skinny lad of eighteen,
with light hair and intense blue eyes, who sailed from
Queenstown on the White Star liner *Celtic* and landed in
New York on August 20, 1904. He was in America to study
for the priesthood, he told the inspectors at Ellis Island,
and was on his way to Mount St. Mary's College in
Maryland. Ten years later, after finishing his studies and
being ordained as a Roman Catholic priest, he was working
as an assistant pastor in Omaha, Nebraska, when he started
his life's work with the homeless. He opened a much-

Felix Frankfurter (1882-1965), Justice of
Supreme Court for 23 years, photographed
in his office at Harvard Law School in 1939,
the year he was named to the Court. The
Frankfurters emigrated from Austria in 1894.
(United Press International, Acme)

needed Workingmen's Hotel in Omaha in 1914. Three years
later, with nothing more than a loan of ninety dollars, he
founded the project that was to make his name known all
over the country: Boys' Town for abandoned and neglected
boys of all religious beliefs and races. Father Flanagan's
famous motto was "There is no such thing as a bad boy."
The work he started goes on, and about ten thousand boys
between the ages of ten and sixteen have by now grown up
in the home built for them by this imaginative Irish
immigrant.

Many immigrants were scarcely more than children when
they arrived in this country, completely alone. A Polish boy
called Samuel Goldfish was one. He ran away from home in

Warsaw when he was eleven and arrived alone at Ellis Island as a steerage passenger two years later, in 1896. His first job paid three dollars a week, and his formal education here was simply one year of night school. But the name he took in 1902 when he became an American citizen—Samuel Goldwyn—became famous all over the world. He entered the motion-picture field in 1913 as a partner in the Jesse Lasky Feature Photoplay Company, and his first production was a silent film called *The Squaw Man*. Three years later he formed the Goldwyn Pictures Corporation which became part of Metro-Goldwyn-Mayer. Goldwyn was one of the first producers to hire famous authors to write scripts for Hollywood. He "discovered" Gary Cooper, Dana Andrews, Danny Kaye and Eddie Cantor (who starred in Goldwyn's first sound film, *Whoopee*, in 1930). Goldwyn

Father Edward Flanagan (1886-1948),
Roman Catholic priest and social worker,
photographed in 1940, 23 years after he founded
Boys Town in Omaha, Nebraska. An Irish farm
boy, he was 18 when he came to the U.S. in
1904 to study for the priesthood.
(Library of Congress, Prints & Photographs Division)

Samuel Goldwyn (born 1882), Hollywood
film producer (at left), photographed in 1935 with
2 of his stars: Mary Pickford
(a Canadian immigrant) and Charlie Chaplin
(an immigrant from Britain). Goldwyn ran away from
home in Poland and was only 13 when he reached
Ellis Island, alone, in 1896.
(United Press International, Acme)

won an Academy Award for producing *The Best Years of
Our Lives*, and he remained a director of United Artists
until 1940.

One Russian immigrant has done more to popularize
classical music in American, it has been said, than even the
invention of the record player. He is Sol Hurok, the
theatrical impresario. Solomon was a teen-ager when his
father, a hardware merchant in the South Ukrainian town
of Pogar, gave him a thousand rubles and sent him to learn
the trade in the big city of Kharkov. Rather than face a
life in the hardware business, Solomon ran away to America. With many other Russian emigrants, he was smuggled
across the border into German territory, held for three
weeks in barracks in Hamburg, and finally crammed into

the steerage of an old tub called the *Graf Waldersee.* He still remembers the following twenty-three nights in a rocking hammock, with the foul air "reeking of tar, herring, and unwashed, seasick humanity." In May, 1906, with less than three rubles in his pocket, staggering under the weight of two hampers of clothes and a big goose-feather pillow, Hurok was admitted through Ellis Island. Because he wanted to live in the city where the Declaration of Independence was signed, he went to Philadelphia and sold sewing needles, drove streetcars, washed soda bottles and bundled midnight editions of the newspaper. Moving to New York, he found a better job in a hardware store on Chambers Street and at the same time improved his English in night classes at the Educational Alliance. He spent his spare time attending every concert he could possibly afford, waiting in line for hours at the box office of the old Hammerstein Theatre, standing at the back of the balcony through five-hour performances of Wagner. On a small scale, he began to organize musical events himself, such as concerts for workingmen's clubs in Brooklyn.

By the time he was twenty-one, Sol Hurok was renting the old New York Hippodrome and Madison Square Garden. He advertised in foreign-language newspapers, telling readers of all ethnic groups where tickets were being sold in their parts of the town, and instructing them how to reach the theaters. He put his tickets on sale at local groceries, cigar stores and newsstands. Hurok proved that there was a mass market for culture, and for over half a century he has presented to American audiences the stars of the world.

The world of entertainment is one in which many immigrants, like Goldwyn and Hurok, have found fame. Movie magnate Spyros P. Skouras, former president of Twentieth Century-Fox, was a seventeen-year-old Greek insurance clerk when he came through Ellis Island in 1910, to join his older brother. Elia Kazan, author and award-winning director of films and plays, was born to a Greek couple living in hostile Turkey; he was four years old when his mother brought him through Ellis Island in 1913. In 1961, Kazan wrote and directed the film *America*

Sol Hurok (born 1888), impresario of concerts
and ballets. The son of a hardware merchant, he
ran away from home in the Ukraine at the
age of 17, and arrived at Ellis Island alone in 1906.
(Courtesy of S. Hurok Concerts, Inc.)

America, a fictionalized version of his family's escape which
has been praised as the universal story of the millions of
immigrants whose willpower and desire for a free life
carried them to this country.

A few months after the teenaged Solomon Hurok landed
in New York, a woodcarver and his family from Kaunas,
Lithuania, passed through Ellis Island. They belonged to
the Misnagdim sect of Ashkenazic Jews. One of their five
children, an eight-year-old-boy already gifted at drawing,
was to become famous as one of the outstanding American
artists of this century: his name was Ben Shahn. On that
sunny autumn day in 1906, Hessel and Gittel Lieberman
Shahn took their children from Ellis Island to the Battery
Park, where they ate rolls and drank tea in the ferry house,
and then on to the home of Mrs. Shahn's brother in
McKibbin Street, Brooklyn. Settled in two rooms of a
cold-water tenement flat, Hessel Shahn (who never learned
to speak English) abandoned his ornate woodcarving to
work as a carpenter. Young Ben was sent off to school, but

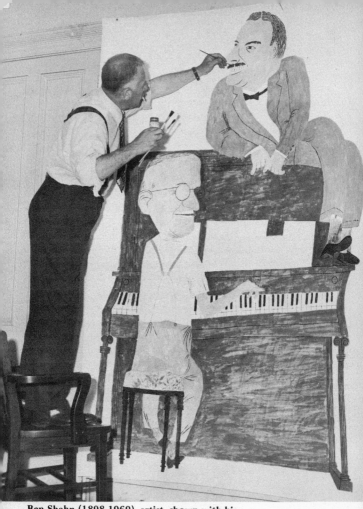

Ben Shahn (1898-1969), artist, shown with his poster lampooning President Harry S. Truman and New York Governor Thomas E. Dewey, done for the Progressive Party Presidential candidate Henry Wallace during the election campaign of 1948. Born to a family of Jewish woodcarvers in Kaunas, Lithuania, Shahn was a child of 8 when he came through Ellis Island on September 29, 1906. *(Wide World Photos)*

he soon devoted his full attention to art; from 1913 to 1917 he attended high school at night and worked during the day as a lithographer's apprentice. He studied drawing at New York University and City College, and later moved on to art classes at the National Academy of Design and the Art Students' League.

Like many Americans, Shahn was convinced that the execution of Nicola Sacco and Bartolomeo Vanzetti in 1927 was the result of prejudice. Regarding the two Italian immigrants as martyrs to injustice, he portrayed their trial and fate in twenty-three paintings which brought him national attention when they were exhibited in the early 1930's. A few years later, Shahn completed a series on Tom Mooney, the labor leader who was convicted of a 1916 bomb killing and pardoned in 1939.

The paintings that Shahn produced often told a story, and they frequently supported liberal causes. In his choice of subjects, he became more "American" than many artists born in the United States. In 1938 Shahn and his second wife, Bernarda Bryson, painted a comprehensive picture of American life on thirteen panels in the Bronx Central Annex Post Office. For the Social Security Building in Washington, D.C., he portrayed the nation's workers in factories and on farms, and he commemorated immigrant garment workers in another mural in the community center of Roosevelt, New Jersey.

Unusually versatile, Shahn became well known for his lectures on art, and for his lithographs, photographs and book designing. His work appeared on book jackets, in posters and advertisements, as well as museums. He used his art in the service of government bureaus and labor organizations, drawing posters for the Office of War Information and for the C.I.O. A social realist whose art is suffused with sympathy for mankind, Ben Shahn has been called "one of the most authentic and powerful of American humanists."

Four years after Shahn's arrival, seven hundred steerage passengers crowded the deck of the Red Star liner *Lapland*, gaping at the outline of Manhattan, just visible through the late afternoon mist. Because it was Christmas Eve—December 24, 1910—they had to wait until the holiday was over

David Dubinsky (born 1892), former
president of the International Ladies' Garment
Workers Union, calling for a strike of
dressmakers in the 1950's. The son of a Polish
baker, David was sent to Siberia for union
organizing, escaped, and fled to
America in 1911. Photo by Harry Rubenstein.
*(Courtesy of International Ladies' Garment
Workers Union)*

before being ferried to Ellis Island. Two of the young men,
David and Chaim Dobniewski from the Russian zone of
Poland, were in such exuberant spirits that they didn't
mind the frustrating wait. David, then nineteen, was the
youngest of nine children born to Bezalel Dobniewski, a
baker in the city of Lodz. Four years earlier, when young
David was secretary of the Jewish bakers' union there, he
had been arrested by the Czar's police (union organization
was forbidden), released after a bribe, then rearrested in
1909 and sent to Siberia for a prison sentence. He managed
to escape and return home to collect his brother Chaim,
who was on the point of being conscripted into the army.
The two brothers walked to a border village where, on the
shrewd advice of local Jewish elders, they bribed the Polish
guard two rubles to look away while they crossed to
German soil.

David, who on his arrival in New York simplified his name to David Dubinsky, still remembers the voyage from Antwerp as "very horrible." His brother Chaim, who lay in the bunk above him, was violently seasick. Meals, served at a long table seating sixty people, consisted often of unpleasantly lukewarm soup. Ellis Island, on the other hand, is still "a happy memory." Dubinsky recalls "the mass of immigrants, the inspection, the overcrowding," but he says, "The idea that I am already in the United States compensated for everything—anything didn't look bad at that time any more!" A man from the Hebrew Immigrant Aid Society was on hand to help, but all David had to do was show his twenty-eight dollars and answer a few simple questions ("Ever been in prison?"—"No," said David, his gray eyes looking straight at the inspector). Then he and Chaim were released into the welcoming arms of two other brothers, Godel and Chone, already living in New York. "When I came down," Dubinsky remembers, "I didn't know what world I'm in . . . I was free! I could go!" They went to the brothers' flat at 14 Clinton Street on the Lower East Side, then one of them rushed out at once to Rivington Street to replace David's torn trousers with a three-dollar secondhand suit.

A few weeks later the neighborhood was stunned by news of the Triangle Factory fire, in which about 145 immigrant girls sewing "shirtwaists" were trapped and killed. Working as a cloak-cutter for three dollars a week, David took out his first membership in the cutters' local of the International Ladies' Garment Workers Union, rose rapidly through the union hierarchy, and became its president in 1932. Dubinsky expanded the I.L.G.W.U.'s membership and scope of operations, and became a national figure and outspoken supporter of the New Deal (invited on occasion to dine with President Roosevelt in the White House). In the 1940's he helped to found the Liberal Party and the Americans for Democratic Action. This immigrant has been called one of America's "giants of justice."

He is one of the millions of immigrants who made the United States a better place by their decision to live and work here.

VI
The
Closing Door
[1914-1932]

In August, 1914, several weeks after a Serbian nationalist assassinated the heir to the imperial throne of Austria-Hungary, the Great War broke out in Europe. Russia backed Serbia's bid for expansion, and the conflict was on, eventually involving almost every nation on the continent. Emigrants trying to leave the Russian and Austro-Hungarian realms found their borders sealed at once. The escape routes from other countries were shut when British ships blockaded the German ports of Hamburg and Bremen, and the former flood of immigrants arriving in New York was abruptly reduced to a trickle. From 878,052 admitted through that port in the fiscal year of 1914, the number fell to less than a quarter the following year: 178,416 in 1915. German submarines began prowling through the shipping lanes of the Atlantic, and after the

A doctor of the U.S. Public Health Service
listens to the heart and lungs of an immigrant
girl during the early years of World War I. As the
number of arrivals continued to drop and
medical requirements became increasingly strict,
1 physician would examine no more than 20 people a day.
*(National Archives, Public Health Service Files,
Photo 90-G-22D-8)*

British *Lusitania* was sunk without warning off the Irish coast, unrestricted submarine warfare was declared. Steamship owners realized that the passage to America had become too dangerous to risk under any flag, even with the most profitable cargoes. So would-be emigrants of all nationalities found themselves trapped to endure the sieges and horrors of the most ghastly conflict in history: at least ten million soldiers and civilians died, and twice that number were wounded. Those who survived faced starvation and epidemic diseases. The few who somehow managed to cross the sea to safety during those terrible years dropped steadily in number: 28,867 immigrants reached New York in 1918, and only 26,731 the following fiscal year—a number that would once have passed through Ellis Island in four or five days.

The great Registry Hall often looked deserted during this period. Since there was no need for their services, many inspectors and employees were transferred to other stations or given long leaves of absence. There were other changes, too, made by a new commissioner, Dr. Frederic C. Howe, appointed by President Woodrow Wilson (who was once Howe's professor at Princeton) just as the war began. The flow of immigrants dried up almost as soon as Howe took the post. Unexpectedly finding spare time on his hands, Howe used it to introduce some human warmth into Ellis Island's efficiency. He told a reporter for *Outlook* magazine (October 21, 1914) that he had been "struck by the dreadful idleness of these poor people" as soon as he had come to the Island. "Some three hundred of them were detained here, compelled to sit hour after hour on hard benches in a bare room, women and children in one, husbands and fathers and sons in another, the length of the building apart, never meeting except at meals, and with absolutely nothing to do." Howe ordered old wooden benches brought out of storage and set around on the lawns, so that detained immigrants (many of them homesick for their farmlands) could look at the sun and grass again. He built an outdoor playground complete with swings for the children, and hired a kindergarten teacher to run it. The Baggage and Dormitory Building's enclosed porch overlooking Manhattan was turned into a day room where families could pass the time together, look at magazines and pictures, and even listen to a gramophone. Band concerts were held on Sunday afternoons, and Howe thought of adding folk dancing. "No one ever seemed to try to imagine what a detained immigrant must be feeling," he grumbled, and to make sure that those feelings now had a chance of expression, he placed small suggestion boxes around the station. At the same time, he improved morale among his employees by reorganizing them in a more democratic way, and inviting them to offer suggestions and hear guest speakers at weekly staff meetings.

In spite of Howe's imagination and good will, the months passed with monotonous slowness for the immigrants being held on the Island for deportation. These were the "undesirables," who, because of poor health or other reasons, could not be admitted into the United States—but neither could they be sent home, as long as all the passenger ships were trapped in port. The boredom of the immigrants' days was broken by Commissioner Howe's musical entertainments and by the occasional arrivals of ferryboats bringing new deportees to join them. The new arrivals were often men and women rounded up from various parts of the country on the charge that they were procurers or prostitutes, and sentenced to deportation under the "white slavery" clause of the immigration laws. As anti-European feelings ran high in America during the war years, this law was sometimes used as little more than an excuse for getting rid of unwelcome immigrants. Arrests and sentencings were carried out without regard for the Bill of Rights or due process of the law. Howe quickly discovered that many of the women in his custody were not professional prostitutes at all, and he succeeded in getting some of the casual offenders released on parole. This action was seized upon by the growing number of his enemies (several of Howe's earlier reforms had threatened to remove money from the tills of the restaurant concessionaires, railroads, steamship lines and local hoteliers), who accused him of being a Socialist and a dangerous innovator: one angry lawyer called him "a half-baked radical with free love

Free sewing materials were provided for detained women by Commissioner Howe to relieve their boredom. Toys, foreign-language newspapers and educational classes were also available for adults and children. By 1926, when Lewis Hine took this photograph, some classes were conducted by the D.A.R.
(Culver Pictures)

ideas."

The tedium of Ellis Island was abruptly shattered around two o'clock on the morning of July 30, 1916, when a nightmare of horror began. A series of tremendous explosions rocked the darkness at New Jersey's Black Tom wharves, just west of Bedloe's Island. German saboteurs had managed to set fire to crates of munitions which were stacked on the docks there and on eighteen surrounding barges in readiness for shipment to Russia (a country then hard at war with Germany on the Eastern Front). Blasts from the detonating ammunition went on for several hours as the flames spread. In New Jersey's nearby towns and as far uptown in Manhattan as Times Square, plate glass windows shattered, residents fled into the streets and vandals looted unprotected stores. Every ambulance in the area rushed toward the pillar of fire lighting up the sky, where seven of the Black Tom warehouses were going up in flames and dozens of people lay injured.

On Ellis Island, less than a mile away, burning debris showered down on the buildings and started many small fires, as hysterical immigrants were led out of dormitories and hospitals. Glass splintered, doors jammed and sections of roofs caved in as the explosions shook the ground, and the night air was alive with screams and the whine of detonating shells. The safest place seemed to be the open tennis courts on the southeast end of Island Number Two, on the Manhattan side of the general hospital. The crowd huddled there was joined by the insane patients, wrapped in blankets and carried out of the psychopathic ward. Then strange shouts of a different kind mingled with the others' cries of terror. "When we had them out of doors, they presented one of the most extraordinary spectacles I have ever seen," reminisced one of the doctors about his deranged patients. "As the five-inch shells flared over the Island like skyrockets, the poor demented creatures clapped their hands and cheered, laughed and sang and cried, thinking it was a show which had been arranged for their particular amusement." They had to be consoled when the explosions finally ended, but the other panic-stricken patients and detainees wanted only to put distance between themselves and danger: they fought for space on the ferry that drew up to take them to the Barge Office. They were in much greater danger than they imagined, for flames had severed the hemp ropes mooring several of the munitions barges to the Black Tom wharves, and the rising westerly wind and incoming tide now carried two of these vessels over to Ellis Island, where they set fire to the wooden cribwork supporting the old seawall. Tongues of flame were nearing the crates of shells and powder on board. The whole Island was saved from being blown up only by the extraordinary heroism of the crews manning tugboats of the Lehigh Valley Railroad, who risked their lives by towing the flaming barges out to sea, "where they sank," wrote a witness, "amid concussions which sounded like the end of the world."

In the light of morning, Ellis Island took stock of its damage. The amazing fact that no one had been seriously injured made one sightseeing journalist report that he was "treading ground where a miracle has been wrought." (Some sort of magic did seem to protect the Island's inhabitants, all of whom had escaped from the fire of 1897 and from a dynamite explosion on Communipaw's Pier Seven in February, 1911—on that second occasion the immigrants had just filed into the dining hall, where they were sheltered from the flying glass as the north side of the Registry Hall blew in.) Over six hundred people had been sleeping on the vulnerable Island when the explosions began—125 nurses and other employees, 353 immigrants in the main building's dormitories, 90 patients in the general hospital and 39 in the contagious-disease wards on Island Number Three. Two patients and two nurses had been slightly cut, but the only serious harm befell Chief Clerk Augustus Sherman's office pet, a cat, which was hit by flying glass. One other pet, a rabbit belonging to a nurse, was seen sitting safely on a case of unexploded powder, licking its fur clean of molasses that had poured over it during the uproar. The damage to property was estimated at $400,000. Windows, tiles, doors, locks and hinges were missing from every building, and so was the roof of the main building. The grounds were littered with broken glass, charred debris and shrapnel. It looked as if a battle had been fought there.

War did come closer to the nation on April 6, 1917, when the United States joined Britain, France, Russia and their allies in declaring war on the forces of Germany, Austria-Hungary and the Ottoman Empire. The first troops of the American Expeditionary Force, commanded by General Pershing, sailed for France that June. Suddenly trapped on this side of the Atlantic were a number of German merchant ships, whose crews, arrested in the harbors of New York and New London, were sent to Ellis Island. There were so many of these newcomers—about 1,150 officers and sailors—that all the quarters in the Baggage and Dormitory Building had to be given over to them. The interned Germans had to be kept under stricter watch than the detained immigrants, so the War Department sent a detachment of soldiers to serve as a military guard; barracks space for them was made on the ground floor of the same building. As outside floodlights and stockades went up, Ellis Island began to look more like a prison, but its inmates were well treated. The German sailors were reported to have suffered only from boredom and the lack of beer.

As the war dragged on, the sailors were joined by other "enemy aliens" arrested by the Justice Department, by the army, and even by the Immigration Service itself, as suspected spies and saboteurs. All together, about 2,200 Germans were interned on the Island during the war. By the spring of 1918, however, other wartime activities on the Island crowded out these prisoners, and they were transferred to camps in North Carolina, Georgia and other states. The navy had appropriated the entire Baggage and Dormitory Building, as well as some space in the main building, to house enlisted men waiting for assignments to American ships then shuttling troops and supplies to Europe. Ellis Island was officially known as Embarkation Number One. The army took over all the hospital buildings that March, and then—noting how easily the new red tile floor in the repaired Registry Hall could be cleaned—converted that into another hospital ward for shell-shocked and wounded doughboys. The Immigration Service itself retreated into such small quarters that it had to inspect the few arriving aliens on board the ships or at the piers.

Many Americans were happy to see the flow of immigrants cut off. The fears and suspicions bred by war led to widespread xenophobia, or hatred of foreigners, accompanied by serious racism at home. Revived in Georgia in 1915, the Ku Klux Klan directed its venom at immigrant Jews and Catholics as well as American-born Negroes, asserting in a publication called *The Fiery Cross* that "Jews dominate the economic life of the nation, while the Catholics are determined to dominate the political and religious life." The Klan voiced the apprehension of "old stock Americans ... that the vast alien immigration is, at the root, an attack upon Protestant religion with its freedom of conscience, and is therefore a menace to American liberties." In the year of the rebirth of the Klan

A man suspected of being feeble-minded
wrestles with a construction puzzle, one of several
tests introduced at Ellis Island in 1913 to
avoid pitfalls of verbal communication with
immigrants from varying cultures. During this period,
about 100 immigrants were refused admission
each month because of mental deficiencies.
*(National Archives, Public Health Service Files,
Photo 90-G-22D-10)*

(soon to reach a membership of five million), public opinion across the United States was outraged at the brutal lynching of young Leo Frank, a Jewish resident of Atlanta. But many Americans who would never have attacked anyone agreed with the racist ideas in the phenomenally popular book *The Passing of the Great Race,* published in 1916 by Madison Grant, an anthropologist at The American Museum of Natural History. Grant regretted that America was no longer the exclusive preserve of descendants of its original northern European settlers—namely the British, Germans and Scandinavians—and he thought the "sentimentalism" that led to emancipation had created a bad precedent. "The agitation over slavery was inimical to the Nordic race," he wrote, "because it thrust aside all national opposition to the intrusion of hordes of immigrants of inferior racial value...." Ignoring the laws that excluded undesirable immigrants, Grant sent shivers of horror through his Anglo-Saxon readers by asserting that "European governments ... unload upon careless, wealthy and hospitable America the sweepings of their jails and asylums." The "new" immigration of Latins, Slavs and Jews consisted, in his eyes, of "a large and increasing number of the weak, the broken and the mentally crippled of all races drawn from the lowest stratum of the Mediterranean basin and the Balkans, together with hordes of the wretched, submerged populations of the Polish Ghettos. Our jails, insane asylums and almshouses are filled with this human flotsam and the whole tone of American life, social, moral and political has been lowered and vulgarized by them." No matter how Americanized the newcomers became, they would always be a threat to Grant: "These immigrants adopt the language of the native American, they wear his clothes, they steal his name and they are beginning to take his women, but they seldom adopt his religion or understand his ideals...."

Thousands of readers absorbed the bigotry of this reputed scientist, and shuddered when they foresaw that the end of the Great War would bring another wave of uprooted refugees, many of them maimed emotionally or physically by their recent sufferings. Organizations like the

Immigration Restriction League, headquartered in New England, began to issue a greater number of speeches and articles insisting that mass immigration be stopped. The United States could not absorb another "flood of the ignorant and unwashed," from southern and eastern Europe in particular, they argued. Their efforts—combined with those of labor organizations anxious to cut off an unending flow of competitors for industrial jobs—were successful.

In 1917 a new immigration law, which President Wilson tried in vain to veto, was passed to keep out as many of these unwelcome would-be citizens as possible. The law specified thirty-three classes of foreigners who would not be admitted, and the most devastating new classification of "undesirables" was a clause excluding illiterates—people over sixteen years old who could not read thirty or forty test words in their own language or dialect. Several previous attempts had been made to reduce the number of immigrants by insisting that they be able to read and write. Twenty years earlier one literacy test had actually been approved by Congress, but vetoed by President Grover Cleveland. Congressional votes had defeated similar bills in 1898, 1902 and 1906 and when two literacy-test acts did pass both the House and the Senate in 1913 and 1915, they were vetoed by Presidents Taft and Wilson. Now public hostility toward aliens was too strong to be held back. Woodrow Wilson argued without success that the legislation would destroy America's image as a land of freedom: it was unfair, he protested to Congress, that "those who come seeking opportunity are not to be admitted unless they have already had one of the chief of the opportunities they seek, the opportunity of education." The literacy test was merely restrictive, not selective, since it excluded "those to whom the opportunities of elementary education have been denied, without regard to their character, their purposes, or their natural capacity." Wilson vetoed the bill, but his veto was overridden by a hostile Congress, and the new Immigration Act became law on February 5, 1917, to stay on the books until 1952.

Two months later the United States abandoned neutrality and entered the war. Thousands of immigrants long settled in this country suddenly found themselves the objects of national hatred, stirred up by a jingoistic press and patriotic speeches made to sell war bonds. Some of the newcomers, wanting to keep the familiar horrors of war out of the New World, had remained pacifist longer than advisable. At first, other groups of immigrants had had good reasons of their own for sympathizing with the "enemy"—Irish-Americans wanted to see the English defeated; all Jews loathed the anti-Semitism of imperial Russia and appreciated Germany's enlightenment; and many German-Americans had admired their fatherland's nationalistic policies. Once the United States joined in the conflict, all "hyphenated Americans" rallied to support and fight for their adopted government, but many of them were suspected of potential treason because of their old loyalties. The American ambassador in London set the tone for many of his countrymen when he suggested they "hang our Irish agitators and shoot our hyphenates and bring up our children with reverence for English history and in the awe of English literature."

The reverence for English history was carried so far that one federal judge banned a film about the American Revolution, entitled *The Spirit of 1776*, saying that any derogatory statement about the British was a violation of the Espionage Act. Other sabotage and sedition acts killed the right of free speech by outlawing "disloyal, profane, scurrilous, or abusive" language about the American government. Some towns fined elderly immigrants who spoke German in public, and the Lutheran Church, condemned as "un-American," was forced to stop holding services in any foreign language, even Swedish, Danish or Norwegian. Foreign-language newspapers were censored and often banned from the mails. German-Americans sadly disbanded their gymnastic societies and men's choirs in a hopeless effort to demonstrate their patriotism. Patriotic children caught "Liberty Measles." All forms of German culture fell into disrepute, and John Philip Sousa was asked to compose new wedding marches to replace the music of the "Huns," Mendelssohn and Wagner. Volumes by German authors were removed from library shelves across the country, and

From a peddler's pushcart decorated with
Allied flags, immigrants on New York's Orchard
Street in 1918 buy war savings-stamps and

certificates. Many of these "hyphenated Americans"
suffered because of the xenophobic hysteria that
gripped longer-established Americans.
(United Press International)

one new history textbook was attacked for including a picture of Frederick the Great.

Tolerance did not return with peace, however. As the fighting stopped, political upheavals occurred in many European cities, where masses of starving, disorganized men clamored for food, work and governmental reforms. Nine new nations struggled for existence. Americans watched in horror as Czarist Russia fell to the Bolsheviks and a new fear gripped this country—the terror of a Red revolution. A special law, enacted a few weeks before the armistice, called for the "exclusion and expulsion of all United States aliens who are members of the anarchist and similar classes." This act paved the way for a shameful episode in American history, the deportation of numbers of perfectly innocent immigrants during the "Red Scare" of 1919.

The new fear was part of the aftermath of war, which brought a feeling of disillusionment and defeat to America. It became clear that the sacrifices of fighting had not made the world "safe for democracy," as Wilson had promised. Europe was in turmoil. At home, Americans faced unemployment, collapsing farm prices, an oppressively high cost of living and a lack of housing in the recently expanded working-class districts of the cities. Race riots erupted in twenty-six cities in 1919, and that year eighty-three Negroes, several of them soldiers in uniform, were lynched. There was deep bitterness among workingmen at political corruption and repression, as gangsters began to profit from Prohibition, and the steel industrialists, using every means to crush 300,000 striking workers, set out to break the power of the A.F.L. forever. The steel strike, said the mill-owners, was "not based upon specific grievances, but is aimed at the overthrow of American institutions and ideals just as surely as if a Bolshevist army was marching on Washington." Many Americans believed them. But the radical wing of the labor movement, fighting wage cuts and mass layoffs, went to the other extreme, and urged anarchy and destruction of capitalism. When more strikes (including one by Boston's policemen) and some mysterious bombings afflicted several cities, the government leaped into action.

In Seattle, a large group of "Wobblies," members of the

left-wing International Workers of the World, were arrested in February, 1919, and sent by train to Ellis Island, where no lawyers were allowed to see them. In New York, police raided the headquarters of the Union of Russian Peasant Workers of America and arrested several men and women there. Immediate deportation was ordered for members of any group advocating violence or overthrow of the government, and the principle of guilt-by-association replaced normal American legal standards. People were arrested for their political opinions, not their actions, and among the supposed anarchists and radicals were laborers whose prime offenses were that they tried to form trade unions, or that they had been born in Russia. The raids and arrests were made without warrants and bail was denied.

Commissioner Howe, returning from the Paris Peace Conference in March, was horrified at what was happening. Refusing to rush the arrested immigrants onto the first available ship, he insisted that every one of them should be given a fair hearing, and he got many of them released on bail. Angry attorneys began to revive accusations that Howe himself was a Socialist or even a Red, and one Congressman demanded his impeachment. Howe succeeded in delaying deportation for one group of immigrants whom he believed would certainly be killed if they were sent back to a homeland devastated by war and currently undergoing violent revolutions—but he arrived at Ellis Island one morning to discover that this agreement with the Secretary of Labor had been broken: the immigrants were being deported at once. Furious, Howe went to Washington for an angry meeting with his superiors. Discovering that the highest officials in the department were being swept up in the hysteria, he handed in his resignation. Howe's critics, rejoicing in his departure, once again attacked his idealism and the changes he had made, claiming that he had turned Ellis Island into "a Socialist Hall, a spouting-ground for Red revolutionists, a Monte Carlo for foreigners only, a club where Europe's offscourings are entertained at American expense. . . ."

Mass arrests began again in November, 1919, instigated by the ambitious Attorney General, A. Mitchell Palmer,

Armed police on patrol pass strikers' houses
in one of Pennsylvania's mill towns in 1919. Strikes
across the nation made Americans fear a
Red revolution. Radical leftists (many of whom were
believed to be immigrants) were blamed.
(Culver Pictures)

whose own house had been bombed. A few weeks after Howe's departure, Ellis Island was filled with arrested immigrants. Among the crowd was the fifty-year-old Russian-born anarchist, Emma Goldman, whose biography is included in Chapter V. She later described the events on Ellis Island at this time in her memoirs. Every day the Island received scores of new deportees from all over the country, many of them without spare clothes or money. Some had been held in local jails for months. Emma complained that innocent immigrants who were not revolutionaries were "treated like felons," "photographed, fingerprinted, and tabulated like convicted criminals," kept in congested quarters on the Island and fed "abominable food." She herself was locked into a small room with two factory workers—one of them a girl barely eighteen years old—who had been arrested in the raid on the Union of Russian Workers. At night, while her roommates kept watch for the guards, Emma wrote a pamphlet deploring the deportations; during daytime walks outside, she was able to discuss the writing with her friend Alexander Berkman, before slipping the pamphlet to visitors who smuggled it off the Island.

Unexpectedly, at midnight on Saturday, December 20, all the detained immigrants were ordered from their rooms, some so quickly that they did not have minutes enough to collect their belongings. Some of them had just been promised a review of their cases and others were expecting to be released on bail pending final decisions, but without exception they were all lined up in the halls, then marched under armed guard at 4 A.M. to a waiting ferry. As that chilly Sunday morning dawned, they were transferred to the *Buford,* a chartered army transport ship; it took them to Finland, where they were sent by train, guarded by soldiers, to the Russian border. Among this group of 249 exiles were many men whose wives and children were left behind, and a few teen-age girls whose families, being too poor to travel long distances to New York, had not seen them since their arrests. Many of the group, brought to America as babies, spoke not one word of Russian. The following month, over four thousand more immigrants were arrested (many without warrants, in spite of legal protests) in raids on the headquarters of labor groups across the United States; six hundred of them from the New York area were held on Ellis Island for deportation, but most were eventually freed. Not until the spring of 1920 did the "Red Scare" wane and the wholesale deportations cease.

By that time, steerage passengers were being received at Ellis Island again, and soon they began to outnumber the departing exiles. In spite of the new restrictions and the literacy test, arrivals in New York—225,206 in 1920, and 560,971 the next year—rapidly approached the prewar rate. The new arrivals found Ellis Island at its shabbiest, and *The New York Times* (September 25, 1920) complained that conditions were "actually worse than during the record immigration before the war." Since much of the dormitory

The anarchist who tossed a bomb at the home of U.S. Attorney General A. Mitchell Palmer (shown here) made a serious error of judgment. Palmer ordered police raids on labor unions across the country and in the winter of 1919 Ellis Island was filled with immigrants sentenced to deportation as political radicals.
(Culver Pictures)

The Buford, an Army transport chartered to serve as the "Soviet Ark," sailed from Ellis Island at dawn on December 21, 1919, deporting 249 Russian-born anarchists and labor unionists to the Soviet Union. Most famous among this group of exiles were Emma Goldman and her friend Alexander Berkman.
(Library of Congress, Prints & Photographs Division, Bain Collection)

and hospital space was still occupied by groups of deportees and by foreign seamen who were now held on the Island for medical treatment, there was a shortage of room. Through the spring and summer of 1920, about five thousand new immigrants arrived every day, and steamships in the harbor were once again forced to keep them for hours, or even days, while the station was cleared. A larger proportion of immigrants than before was detained on the Island, sometimes for many weeks, partly because of the stricter admission requirements, but largely because so many of them from war-torn countries arrived as penniless refugees who had to be held until funds or friends came. Into a detention day room built for four hundred, one thousand immigrants might be crammed. More than three thousand were sometimes bedded down—two in a bunk, many on blankets spread on the floor—in dormitories meant for half their number. The perennial complaint was heard that detained cabin-class passengers had to share quarters with uncouth peasants. The English in particular—in letters to the *Times* of London and in speeches in the House of Commons—objected vociferously to the fact that their citizens were "inhumanly kept in cages with people of dirtier and inferior nationalities." The British ambassador was sent to investigate and subsequently proposed an enormous new main building with separate inspection facilities and dormitories for every nationality (". . . the place would look like a honeycomb," protested the commissioner).

Ellis Island, however, did not have the staff to run the buildings it had. The old employees, experienced in coping with much larger crowds than current, had been dispersed by the war and only partly replaced with new men, who were less efficient and disciplined. Examinations were so detailed that they took much longer: forty overworked doctors each tried to inspect one hundred immigrants every day, but new procedures made it impossible to check more than twenty properly. The dining-hall employees, often called upon to produce meals for three thousand, some days could do no more than hand out coffee and sandwiches to the waiting immigrants. The aging buildings they worked in, given hard use during the war, had not been properly rehabilitated before the new wave of refugees began to crowd in. Even the maintenance men could no longer cope—floors and walls everywhere were filthy and covered with vermin. The editors of *The New York Times* (December 14, 1920) declared the facilities were "a disgrace as well as a danger to the country."

All steerage bunks were now sold a year in advance, the steamship lines announced in August, 1920. The literacy test had turned out to be no barrier at all, proving, as Professor Oscar Handlin has sarcastically commented, that "even the inferior races, if they had to, could learn to

These Spanish laborers, photographed on
Ellis Island's recreation ground, typified the
southern Europeans whom many Americans at
that time wanted to keep out, believing

them to be "of inferior racial value."
These men would have had to pass the literacy test
introduced in 1917. Photo by Paul Thompson, 1920.
(New York Public Library, Picture Collection)

read." By the last week in September, the overcrowding was so bad that there were near-riots on the Island and on the landing barges, and the inspection of new immigrants was temporarily halted until the congestion was relieved. The newly appointed commissioner, Frederick Wallis, hurried down to Washington, demanding that the laborious inspection procedures be temporarily suspended, and asking for a five-million-dollar construction program. He complained, incidentally, that the literacy test kept out honest and sturdy workers while educated criminals slipped by. Congress, in the midst of a national battle over more stringent restrictions on all immigration, was in no mood to make procedures more lenient or to authorize money, even for repairs. The Committee on Immigration and Naturalization was simply authorized to "study the situation." Back on Ellis Island, doctors and inspectors struggled with the situation that daily became worse. On December 29, when 1,050 immigrants had been virtually imprisoned on the *Olympic* for six days at great cost to the shipping line, special permission was sent from Washington for those inspections to take place on the pier. This exception to normal procedure was to be made on many occasions during the next six months, until a new law abruptly reduced the number of arriving immigrants.

Since the literacy test had failed to discourage enough immigrants, another means was used. The so-called First Quota Law was signed in May, 1921, by President Warren Harding almost as soon as Wilson (who had vetoed it) was out of the White House. The law imposed an absolute numerical limit to European immigration. The United States would admit no more from each nation than the equivalent of 3 per cent of their countrymen who had been living here in 1910. An annual ceiling of 358,000 immigrants was imposed. This system meant that the largest quotas went to the "oldest" immigrant groups, while the number allowed from southern and eastern Europe would be slashed to a tiny fraction of the prewar levels. This national discrimination in favor of the "Nordic race" was the main purpose of the law, and it marked a turning point in American policy, establishing a discriminatory principle that was not abolished until 1965.

The First Quota Law, or Johnson Act, which went into effect on June 3, 1921, specified that no more than 20 per cent of a nation's quota could be filled in any one month. Officials of the shipping companies were close to panic; during the last few days of grace they organized a mad dash to land thousands of immigrants in American ports before the deadline. Any ship that could make the transatlantic passage was crammed with passengers and some vessels racing through the Narrows actually collided in their haste. During June, once the new system was in effect, steamships still raced to land their passengers on Ellis Island as soon as possible, and within the first few days of the month the specified 20 per cent of all national quotas had been filled. Then the first scenes of a human tragedy began. Some ten thousand aliens arrived at Ellis Island to be told that their quotas had been filled for June—there was no room for them in America. It was an impossible situation that no one, apparently, had foreseen. Puzzled officials held the surplus immigrants on their ships and asked Washington for instructions; the answer came back that the immigrants were to be admitted on bond, and their numbers subtracted from July's quotas.

But in July, and during the first days of every succeeding month, the same thing happened, as the steamships continued their race to grab as large a share as possible of the quotas for their own passengers. Whole shiploads of immigrants were now turned back to Europe in scenes of terrible anguish described by one Public Health Service doctor as "one of my most painful reminiscences of service at the Island." She recalled one particular group of five hundred southeastern Europeans who had sold their homes and possessions and traveled four thousand miles to start a new life, only to hear after they had passed the Statue of Liberty that they were inadmissible. "They screamed and bawled and beat about like wild animals, breaking the waiting-room furniture and attacking the attendants, several of whom were severely hurt. It was a pitiful spectacle...." The immigrants were helpless victims of the steamship lines, and the immigration inspectors were helpless too, in the

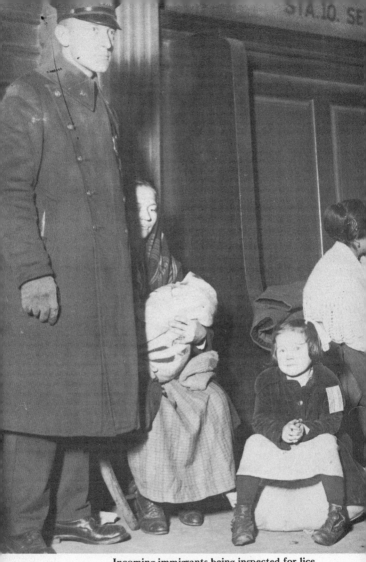

Incoming immigrants being inspected for lice
in 1921. Although a familiar insect at Ellis Island,
the body louse was now seen for the
first time as a national health hazard, as it spread
typhoid fever across war-torn Europe.

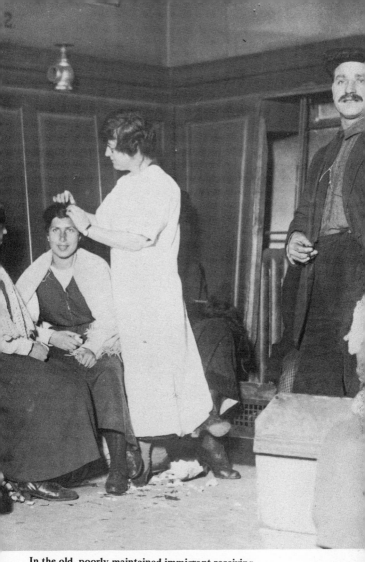

In the old, poorly maintained immigrant receiving
station, so many vermin were found on the
dirty floors and walls that 1 doctor announced, "I
would declare Ellis Island an infected port."
(Culver Pictures)

face of the new law. Commissioner Wallis complained bitterly to Washington in October, 1921, that "our nation is committing a gross injustice." He urged that immigrants be examined by American consuls in European ports, to save all this "indescribable" suffering "that would melt a heart of granite." Wallis had submitted his resignation as Wilson left the White House, and he was now replaced. The Secretary of Labor, happy to see him go, criticized him privately for "going around telling sob stories designed to discredit the immigration laws."

The Republican appointee who succeeded Wallis was Robert E. Tod, a wealthy Scottish-born banker, yachtsman and philanthropist. When Tod arrived on Ellis Island, he discovered that the Harding administration had already reduced the staff from 780 to 520 employees as part of a national economy campaign. This cutback, combined with the low salaries most government employees were receiving, made the low morale unsurprising. Employees were rude and dishonest, one investigating committee of welfare workers reported; they customarily took bribes from immigrants who, used to similar systems in Europe, offered few complaints. Tod did his best to improve the immigrants' reception. During the winter lull in arrivals, he converted one large storage area into a reception room where immigrants could wait in comfort for their examinations, instead of being held on the landing barges. An information room, complete with cafeteria, was set up for waiting friends and relatives. Detained women with small children were given a bigger day room and a nursery where they received lessons in bathing and clothing babies according to latest American medical practice.

With the coming of spring the crisis resumed, as the steamships' races began again. Around midnight of the last day of every month they would maneuver for space in the Narrows, trying to be the first admitted in the new month when all quotas would have new spaces released. The morale of the overworked, underpaid staff sank lower than ever, while politicians and lawyers wearied Commissioner Tod with pleas for special exceptions to the exclusion laws. Exhausted, he retired to private business in June, 1923,

The Second Quota Law of 1924, based
on the American population of 1890, meant
that this German family was admitted without
difficulty. As Lewis Hine photographed them in
1926, they received railroad tags to their
final destination. Immigrants were then likely to
be white-collar workers, and whereas men had
once outnumbered women 7 to 3, at least
half of the arriving immigrants were then female.
By the 1930's they would outnumber men 6 to 4.
*(New York Public Library, Local History
& Genealogy Division)*

An aerial photograph of Ellis Island,
taken from the south around 1921. Some landfill is
in place in the slip between Islands
No. 2 and 3, foreground. Two ferries are docked in

front of the glass marquee of the main building
on Island No. 1. At top, a railroad barge pulls
away from the dock of the Baggage & Dormitory Building.
(Courtesy of Dr. Thomas Pitkin)

halfway through his second summer, and left his successor, a New York City politician named Henry Curran, to inherit the abuse that seemed inevitably to fall on the head of the Island's unlucky administrator.

One of the chief causes for complaint, apart from overcrowding, was the long time it took for appealed cases to be decided. Some detained immigrants were kept in suspense for weeks, if not months, while their files passed slowly from hand to hand in Washington. Commissioner Curran tried to relieve this problem by transferring more authority into his own hands, and he wrote caustic letters to the Department of Labor blaming the secretary for delays of one to three months. Describing the case of a Mr. and Mrs. Einsiedler who had been detained for five months, he said they had "become so indigenous to the soil of Ellis Island that Mr. Einsiedler has mastered the American game of basketball and is now the leader in alien outdoor sports here. Mrs. Einsiedler," continued Curran, "has been occupied having a baby at Ellis Island. I do not know what will happen next. But I do know that this case could have been decided before this time."

Before the Einsiedlers were released, Ellis Island was over the worst of its problems. The restrictive law and the sad tales of rejection which were taken back to Europe reduced the volume of arrivals; physical improvements were made; and the staff was better organized. The First Quota Law, never intended to be more than a temporary measure, was replaced in July, 1924, by a second, more restrictive act based on the same principle. The basis for the quotas was moved back from the population census of 1910 to that of 1890—cutting still further the proportion of "new" immigrants (who in 1890 were just starting to arrive). The percentage of admissible immigrants from any nation was reduced from 3 per cent to 2 per cent of its population in this older census, and the overall ceiling was slashed from 358,000 to 164,000 people a year. Italy's quota, under this arrangement, was cut from 42,057 under the First Quota Law to a mere 3,845 per year. The second law's most important provision, as far as Ellis Island's history is concerned, was a rule that all immigrants were to be inspected at the American consular offices in Europe, where visas would be issued to those found acceptable. Consuls would slowly fill the national quotas, issuing no more than 10 per cent of the available visas in one month, in an attempt to end the first-come-first-served system used by the steamships and the inevitable disappointments in American ports.

As soon as the second law went into effect, the Secretary of Labor visited Ellis Island and boasted that the place looked "like a 'deserted village.'" Immigrants were still examined there, but they arrived in an evenly spaced flow over the months, and very few of those who had been judged acceptable by the consuls had to be detained. There was now enough time and space for physical conditions on the Island to be rapidly improved: iron bunks were moved out to make room for proper beds with mattresses, and modern plumbing replaced what one magazine writer called the "ancient exhibits." Ellis Island looked like a different place—and it was, because its role was completely changing. In 1926 and 1927, immigration inspectors and Public Health Service doctors were stationed at American consulates over most of Europe, and the primary inspection of the immigrants—once the Island's function—was finished before the immigrants even set sail. Possession of an American visa was almost a guarantee of admission. Inspectors in New York needed only to make a final check of all passengers as the ships sailed into the Upper Bay, and they held only a few doubtful cases—eventually about 1 per cent of all arrivals—for questioning before Boards of Inquiry or for medical treatment. By 1926, much of Ellis Island's staff had been disbanded. Dust began to settle in the empty rooms. In 1928 officials in Washington were acknowledging it to be "something of an economic problem."

The small number of immigrants the Island received was further reduced after July, 1929, by the final revision of the so-called "National Origins" system. The maximum number of all admissions was lowered to about 150,000 a

By the late 1920's, Ellis Island's role as the primary inspection place for immigrants was finished. Those in this photograph, waiting to enter the main building in 1928, were among

year. So that the racial and national mixture of the American people would remain frozen as it was, new quotas were based on an analysis of the national origins of the population, both native and foreign-born, as recorded in the latest census (1920). By the new law's complex calculations (the number of each nationality to be admitted in one year was to bear the same ratio to 150,000 as the number of that national origin in the United States in 1920 bore to the total population then), only 6,524 Polish immigrants could enter in a year, with no more than 2,712 from Russia—but Great Britain's quota, never filled, was an annual 65,721.

the very few doubtful cases whose papers
or health were queried by inspectors on board
ships in the harbor.
*(Library of Congress, Prints & Photographs
Division)*

Emigrants from the unfavored nations had to be prepared
to wait many years, sometimes a lifetime, before they could
apply for a visa. When Wall Street collapsed later in 1929,
the most naive would-be immigrant realized that the New
World's streets were not paved in gold, and that perhaps
there was no good reason to struggle to get into a country
where he was not welcome. By 1932, when admissions
dropped to a low point, immigrants going back to Europe
to escape from the Depression outnumbered those arriving.
The days of the great migration to America were over
forever.

VII
Deportees and
Displaced Persons
[1933-1965]

Once the "golden door" into America, Ellis Island became the nation's chief port of expulsion in the 1930's. The thousands of arrested immigrants deported from the Island far outnumbered the small groups of arriving foreigners (only 4,488 in 1934) who were held there for two or three days while their right to land was investigated. In 1932 the nationwide total of deportations rose to 19,426—over three thousand of whom were sent home from Ellis Island. In addition to the deportees, many more thousands returned to their native lands of their own free will. In 1933, for example, 127,660 people left the United States, while only 23,068 new immigrants arrived.

The disillusioned crowd being deported to Europe was

A soup kitchen in Chicago offers
"free soup, coffee and doughnuts for the unemployed"
in November, 1930.
(United Press International)

made up largely of stowaways, sailors who had jumped ship, immigrants who were illegally smuggled across the borders from Mexico or Canada and foreign visitors who had stayed longer than their visas permitted. More than ever before, Ellis Island at this time deserved its name as the "Island of Tears." In the Registry Hall, men cried and prayed for last-minute help almost as if they had been condemned to die. Scenes of real tragedy occurred nearly every day and a few deportees committed suicide rather than board ship for Europe—one young Italian shot himself on the Island, others drowned in the waters of the harbor or leaped from the transcontinental train (the "Deportation Special" from San Francisco) bringing them to New York. The current commissioner of Ellis Island, an Italian-born social worker named Edward Corsi, confessed that he found "the duties of deportation . . . very bitter." "Our deportation laws are inexorable and in many cases inhuman," he wrote in his memoirs, "particularly as they apply to men and women of honest behavior whose only crime is that they dared to enter the promised land without conforming to law. I have seen hundreds of such persons forced back to the countries they came from, penniless, and at times without coats on their backs. I have seen families separated, never to be united—mothers torn from their children, husbands from their wives, and no one in the United States, not even the President himself, able to prevent it."

These were also unhappy years for those who remained in America, immigrant and native alike. By the end of 1932, three years after the stock market collapse, industry was operating at less than half of its 1929 volume and corporations reported a two-billion-dollar loss that year. More than thirteen million workers were unemployed and bread lines grew longer every day. Some five thousand banks had closed their doors; in many cities, half-built office towers stood rusting like metal skeletons, reminding passersby of the abrupt end to construction and to prosperity. Only the Prohibition bootleggers were getting rich. In 1932 alone, about 250,000 families lost their farms and homes as mortgages went unpaid; the homeless clustered in railroad freight cars and "hobo jungles" in city parks and slums. This was the first of several years in which arriving immigrants were outnumbered by those leaving the land of their unfulfilled dreams.

As the Depression reached its depths, President Hoover welcomed the chance to be rid of all aliens who might compete with American citizens for the dwindling number of jobs. He was delighted to hear from the zealous Secretary of Labor that there were an estimated 400,000 foreigners illegally residing in the country, and thus subject to arrest and deportation. He gave his approval for a campaign to remove them all from American shores. Combing cities for any immigrants who might be classified as anarchists or unemployed vagrants ("likely to become public charges"), police raided dance halls, seamen's hostels, restaurants and any other places where crowds of the foreign-born might gather: those who failed to convince the officers that they had a right to be in the country were hauled off to jail, and from there to Ellis Island. The hearings that led to their final deportation were often prejudiced, since one immigration inspector served as both prosecutor and judge. But many of the immigrants did not care—they wanted to go home. Some of them voluntarily turned themselves in to the authorities, stating that they were penniless (during the worst of the Depression, as many as two hundred people a month took advantage of the rule that destitute aliens who had lived in the United States for less than three years must be shipped home at American expense). A few canny Scotsmen devised a slightly different means of traveling home free: hearing that there might be shipbuilding jobs available on the Clyde, they confessed to the Immigration Service that they were "anarchists" who would have to be deported.

Immigrants returning home were sometimes detained on Ellis Island for many months, while European consuls prepared passports for them or slowly investigated their right to return to their birthplaces. When Corsi became commissioner in November, 1931, he was appalled to see that these deportees were treated like prisoners during their long detention on the Island: they were forbidden to make telephone calls, could receive visitors only on Tuesdays and

Thursdays, and (because of the shortage of guards) were allowed outdoors for only an hour or two each day. Corsi changed the regulations as soon as he could, permitting immigrants to spend most of their time outside—where they paced in the sunshine, played sports, or sat staring listlessly at the buildings of the nearby city they had left forever. He was even successful in persuading his superiors in Washington to halt the mass arrests by police; a legal warrant was henceforth needed before any immigrant could be arrested and fair hearings were held on every case.

Corsi's diplomacy in handling his superiors also led to important physical improvements on Ellis Island: close to $1,500,000 in government funds were appropriated for renovation and new construction, and the last major phase of building on the Island took place in 1934 and 1935.

Although Europeans no longer dreamed of America as a land of unlimited promise, it was not a lack of desire to come here that prevented more of them from immigrating during the 1930's. American policy kept them out. Commissioner Corsi described his main duty as that of guarding the nation's gate: "I would open it, swing it back upon its heavy hinges to allow the passage of the few who had been carefully selected; then slam it shut and turn the keys again." As financial panic gripped the nation, the door was locked against all but the obviously prosperous: in September, 1930, President Hoover ordered American consuls to interpret in the strictest possible sense the law excluding all immigrants "likely to become public charges." As a result, immigration slowed to an almost complete halt—to the approval of many American sociologists who proclaimed that the country's population was already too large for the faltering economy to support.

Economic and political troubles spread across Europe. Adolph Hitler became Chancellor of Germany in 1933, Benito Mussolini of Italy attacked the Ethiopians, and civil war broke out in Spain: the post-Versailles world, which had never recovered from World War I, began to crumble. As the shadow of dictatorship fell across much of the continent, thousands of refugees from persecution—many of them German Jews—besieged American consulates, begging to be admitted to the United States. But their pleas could not soften the American mood of isolationism; the desire to immunize this country from the political involvements of the Old World was so strong that one historian has called it a "national secular religion in the 1930's." The barriers imposed by the quota system did not fall, and many refugees denied American visas were later murdered by Hitler. The 250,000 refugees who did enter the United States between 1933 and 1944 had to produce guarantees that they would not become public charges. Therefore, they came largely from the well-educated and prosperous upper middle class, or under the sponsorship of private welfare agencies, and they came in small numbers. Many of them were Jewish, or—like the German novelist Thomas Mann and the Italian physicist Enrico Fermi—political opponents of fascism. Not since 1848, when the liberal revolution failed in Germany, had so many illustrious intellectuals arrived as refugees in the New World. Their numbers included Protestant theologian Paul Tillich; physicists Albert Einstein, Leo Szilard, Edward Teller and George Gamow; Theodore von Karman, pioneer rocket engineer from Hungary; and literally dozens of psychologists, political scientists, painters, architects, writers and musicians who today are among the United States' most famous citizens. But the talents of those who came here during the "intellectual migration" did not guarantee them a welcome in Depression-struck America, and in many states the refugees faced restrictive laws barring noncitizens from the professions—medicine, law, teaching, accounting and even plumbing.

The continent from which these immigrants had so hastily fled erupted into violence in the autumn of 1939. The Germans, already in control of Austria and Czechoslovakia, invaded Poland from the west, while Russian forces advanced from the east and crossed into Finland. The following spring, Hitler's troops swiftly overran Denmark, Norway, the Netherlands and Belgium; France surrendered in June, 1940, a few days after Italy had joined the conflict on Germany's side. Stunned Americans, realizing that they would face the totalitarian armies alone if

During the Depression, Ellis Island's Registry Hall became a day room for deportees, many of whom spent months there while hearings were held or European consuls investigated their right to return home. These bored men were permitted outdoors for only an hour or two a day. Photo by Dr. Erich Salomon, 1932.
(Magnum Photos)

Britain fell, reassessed their policy of neutrality, voted to conscript men between twenty-one and thirty-five years old, and rushed aid to the British.

Very few passenger ships now crossed the submarine-infested Atlantic, and the early years of the war saw more sailors than immigrants on Ellis Island. The Coast Guard, initially ordered to patrol American waters in this area to enforce the Neutrality Act of 1935, trained and housed its new recruits in a newly built Immigrant Building, as well as on the ground floor of the Baggage and Dormitory Building. On April 12, 1940, these sailors were given a happier task: to fire their cannons in celebration of Ellis Island's birthday—fifty years had passed since President Harrison signed the bill establishing the immigrant receiving station on the Island. The station itself had never been emptier, and Corsi's successor, Commissioner Rudolph Reimer, had little work to do except listen to the Budget Bureau complain about the high cost of maintaining the nearly deserted buildings and unused ferryboat. Reimer's superiors in Washington offered to give the whole Island to the Coast Guard, in exchange for a new building in Manhattan, where all the local operations of the Immigration and Naturalization Service could more conveniently and cheaply have been housed. The new building was actually approved by President Roosevelt's Executive Office, but Congress never appropriated the construction funds, and the project sank from sight in the midst of the government's more urgent wartime activities.

The United States went to war on December 8, 1941, a day after Japanese planes bombed the country's chief Pacific naval and air bases at Pearl Harbor in the Hawaiian Islands. As had happened at the outbreak of World War I, some enemy ships were trapped in American waters, and their crews were temporarily imprisoned on Ellis Island before being sent to other detention camps. Citizens of Germany, Italy and Japan living in many parts of the United States were arrested by the vigilant Federal Bureau of Investigation and sent to the Island for the war's duration. Ellis Island once again became a prison for enemy aliens and their families, who whiled away long years of boredom with card games and handicrafts. Some spent their days slumped on wooden seats in the Registry Hall, staring into space and listening to the echoes. By May, 1942, when a thousand of these unlucky immigrants had accumulated on the Island, overcrowding was so bad that some of them had to be transferred to dormitories on Riker's Island in the East River. To make a little more room, the administrative offices of the Immigration and Naturalization Service were moved the next year to a government-owned office building in Manhattan. The aliens themselves, some of whom spent six or seven years on the Island, lived only for the end of the war and the day of their release.

The fighting ended in the summer of 1945, the Coast Guard left Ellis Island in 1946, and the few remaining guards and detainees could hear their own footsteps echoing in the cold, tiled corridors. The deserted main building, now officially called a "detention facility," was no longer an immigration station even in name. The Island's operating costs were exorbitant. Once again the authorities suggested that the Immigration and Naturalization Service relinquish its ownership, but no other governmental department had any use for the place and the National Park Service had barely enough funds to maintain the historic sites already in its care.

As the wounds of war healed, transatlantic travel slowly resumed—now by airplane to La Guardia Field as well as by ship. One hundred and twenty thousand of the immigrants who entered the country between 1946 and 1952 were European wives of American servicemen, and under the War Brides Act they were exempt from the national quota system, which otherwise remained strictly in force. Two more years passed before the conservative Eightieth Congress was willing to aid a much larger group of Europeans in more serious need of legislative help—many hundreds of thousands of refugees, exiled from their homes and herded into Allied detention camps, were pleading for admission to the United States. After many delays by a stubborn bloc of rural senators, Congress passed the Displaced Persons Act in June, 1948, admitting no more than 205,000 of these refugees. President Truman signed the bill "with very great reluctance," claiming that it was inadequate and "flagrantly discriminatory." (By stipulating that a high percentage of the DP's must be farmers or come from Baltic countries, the act excluded many Jews and Catholics.) Francis Cardinal Spellman, Military Vicar of the Armed Forces, toured Europe and raised his voice at home in support of the President, urging that the immigration laws be revised to admit "starving, suffering peoples." After Truman's surprising reelection in 1948, Congress did pass a new and somewhat liberalized version of the act, raising the total of admissible refugees to 400,000. The nation's gate was at least ajar. Sympathetic immigration administrators and the hard-working agents of American charities did the best they could within the framework of the act. Fewer than 1 per cent of the arriving immigrants (and visitors,

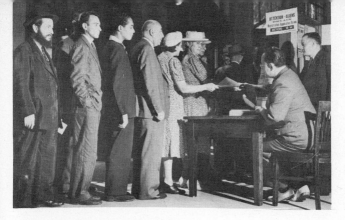

Immigrants living in New York City
in August, 1940, line up in the General Post Office
to collect forms required by the new
Alien Registration Act. Passed that June in the
prewar mood of national isolationism and
insecurity, the law called for all
noncitizens to be identified, fingerprinted and
given an oath of allegiance.
(United Press International, Acme)

The Registry Hall was used during World War II
as the main day room for interned German
families and other "enemy aliens," a few of
whom were held on the Island as late as 1947,
when this picture was taken.
(United Press International, Acme)

who were not distinguished by the law) had to go to Ellis Island while their passports and entry permits were re-examined; the Island's staff, once overworked to the point of exhaustion, now welcomed their few guests almost eagerly.

A sudden rash of detentions broke the monotony in the winter of 1950, when American suspicions about incoming aliens led to a new set of regulations. Ever since the eve of World War II, when the House Committee on Un-American Activities was created, arriving foreigners had been regarded as possible agents of political subversion. Immigrants—once seen as a sort of import to be taxed by the Department of the Treasury, then as workers to be governed by the Department of Labor—were transferred in June, 1940, to the jurisdiction of the Department of Justice as potential threats to national security. Every immigrant who landed in the United States after that date had to submit his finger-prints and police records for careful scrutiny, and those noncitizens already living in the country were required to register with the department. This trend to paranoia reached its peak in 1950 (the year in which Senator Joseph McCarthy rose to power), when the Internal Security Act, sponsored by Communist-hunting Senator Pat McCarran, was passed in defiance of President Truman's veto. The bill—one clause of which barred aliens who had ever belonged to Communist or Fascist organizations—was so loosely phrased that its result was to exclude a far greater number of harmless and hard-working immigrants than those interested in political plots.

As the Truman Administration set out in the winter of 1950 to prove this law unworkable by enforcing it to the letter, many astonished visitors and immigrants who had believed their visas to be in order were hustled off their ships in New York harbor and detained on Ellis Island. Prominent detainees, such as a visiting Austrian concert pianist whose offense had been joining the Hitler Youth when in school, were given the satisfaction of publicity in the newspapers. But most of the bewildered victims of this sudden turn in American politics were unable to understand why they had been detained, and could find no consolations. Many of them were displaced persons, driven from homes invaded by the Nazis or occupied by the Russians; many of them had been compelled to enroll in Fascist or Communist groups in order to attend school, find jobs or collect pensions. On Ellis Island they faced long, baffling delays as they struggled with red tape and endless questions about their wartime activities. The overcrowding was as bad as it had been in the middle of the war, because many of the long-unused dormitories remained closed. To pass the days, the more energetic Europeans played football or ping-pong, or listened to the radio in the recreation room; others, exhausted by this final setback when they had believed that their trials were over, sat silently on the Registry Hall's wooden benches, and waited for more

A Polish woman and her sons laugh with joy
as they disembark from the General Black
in New York in October, 1948. They were among
the first of 400,000 refugees admitted during the
following 4 years under the Displaced Persons Act.
(United Press International, Acme)

interrogations or release. Not until the spring of 1951 did an amendment to the Internal Security Act halt the detention of refugees who had only reluctantly joined proscribed organizations in order to eat and stay alive.

Ellis Island emptied again, but only for a few weeks. The crowding on the Island suddenly became worse than ever in June, 1951, when mass arrests of illegally resident aliens—rounded up in the city's restaurants, bars, hotels and docks—temporarily swelled its unhappy population to fifteen hundred. Detentions rose again after Christmas Eve, 1952, when the controversial McCarran-Walter Act rigidified the quota system and stipulated that even foreign seamen must be screened for their political attitudes before being granted leave in American ports. Dusty filing cabinets were pushed out of day rooms and dormitories that had not been in use for years. The dining-hall staff worked almost all day long to serve meals. Renovations and repairs were made and new furniture was bought, but local administrators continued to complain to Washington that the old station, "with its great, wide halls and corridors, high ceilings, unusable spaces and outmoded utilities," was hard to run with efficiency and economy. Recommendations for a modern, smaller station in Manhattan were simply gathering dust in the files of the Senate Appropriations Committee. But in 1954 someone finally thought of an arrangement whereby all the activities at Ellis Island could be transferred to the Immigration Service's offices at 70 Columbus Avenue, or to the new headquarters under construction on West Broadway. The idea was beautifully simple: all detainees whose papers did not satisfy governmental regulations for some "technical" reason would be freed on a parole system, and only those few who were likely to vanish or to endanger the national security would be locked up in rooms next to the office space. With a stroke of the pen in November, 1954, this policy went into effect. A few days later only ten detainees were left on Ellis Island, and when the last of them—a Norwegian sailor called Peterssen who had missed his ship—was sent home, the Island had said goodbye to its last immigrant. The old gateway, through which some twelve to sixteen million immigrants (no one would ever be quite sure of the figures) had entered the United States, was closed forever. The following March, Ellis Island was officially declared "surplus property."

Optimistically seeking a private commercial buyer in a sealed-bid sale, the General Services Administration advertised the possibilities of the Island, complete with its thirty-five buildings and fixtures (even the ferryboat was included). Ellis Island was tentatively valued at $6,500,000 (the amount it had cost taxpayers to build and run it), but it was rumored that the government would be willing to sell

Over 80 Chinese men, believed to be deserting sailors and "active Communists" according to news reports, were taken to Ellis Island for questioning in January, 1951. For Chinese immigrants—long excluded, denied citizenship or persecuted on the West Coast—the mass arrests of the McCarthy era were nothing new. Immigration inspectors still raid Chinese restaurants, hoping to catch illegal residents.
(United Press International, Acme)

The Stars and Stripes, crumpled across a desk,
once hung in the Registry Hall, offices and
school room, and fluttered from the tall flagpole to
the east of the main building.
(Photo by Joan Redmond)

The Ellis Island had logged over 1 million nautical
miles in 50 years of service, when she made her last
15-minute trip from Manhattan to the
abandoned Island on November 29, 1954.
Pounded by bad weather and waves from passing
ships, she sank at her berth in August, 1968.
*(Courtesy of the National Park Service,
New York Group)*

it for one million dollars—as long as it approved of the use to which the Island would be put.

For nearly ten years, bids and suggestions came in from people who wanted to build a six-hundred-room hotel with a heliport and marina, or an orphanage for foreign children, a women's prison, a seamen's school, a casino, a Bible college, a world trade fair, an International Cathedral for Peace Prayers, even the City of Tomorrow with moving sidewalks. All of these offers—and many others less practical—were rejected. Legislators and citizens (many of them immigrants or their children) increasingly began to protest that Ellis Island should not be sold for any private use at all, but should be preserved as a public monument. There were public hearings in New York City, and in Washington at least five bills concerning the Island's fate were introduced into the Senate.

In September, 1963, subcommittee hearings were held under the chairmanship of Senator Edmund Muskie (son of a Polish tailor named Marciszewski who immigrated in

1903). The following year the National Park Service released a study which concluded that the Island should be handed over to its jurisdiction as a "national historic site." On May 11, 1965, President Lyndon Johnson officially proclaimed the Island a part of Statue of Liberty National Monument. It was saved. Plans were drawn up for preserving the main building and the original hospital within a park.

But nothing could be done without funds for the restoration project, money which Congress authorized but never actually appropriated. The National Park Service was not even granted enough money for the Island's maintenance, and, once the G.S.A.'s watchmen and police dogs had left, the vandals moved in, stealing copper roofing, chandeliers, machinery and plumbing fixtures. Tall weeds and undergrowth invaded the wharves, gravel paths and recreation fields, while large holes appeared in the slowly collapsing seawall. Vines climbed the brick walls and poked through the broken windows. Inside the empty Registry Hall the silence was broken only by the creaking of a wind-blown door, falling lumps of plaster, and the occasional flapping of a pigeon's wings high under the vaulted ceiling. The shoes of a casual visitor kicked up small mementos of the past from the debris of paint flecks, plaster and glass: a rusted key labeled "U.S.P.H.S. Infirmary Linen Room," a railroad ticket stub and an orange plastic badge marked "Ellis Island Commissary Project 229." Some rooms held piles of well-worn mattresses. Abandoned in the library was a dusty set of the sermons of Mary Baker Eddy, in Czech translation. Three khaki army overcoats lay across chairs in the darkened cafeteria, and on the wall, beside a multilingual notice about depositing trays, was posted the final menu, typed by someone with an uncertain command of English spelling: "Supper: Tomato Sauice; Buttered Spagheti, Choped Lettuca." They had eaten this last meal on the Island, washed the dishes and simply locked the door behind them—or so it seemed. The eerie stillness had an air of expectancy about it, as if at any moment the immigrants and employees might return. The Island was waiting.

One footnote to the history of Ellis Island must be

added, because it represents a happy ending to a sad story. At the time the Island was declared a national historic site, Congress was considering a complete revision of the immigration laws which had caused so much grief there. The quota system's bias had been under attack for forty years, ever since it had been established in 1921. As President Truman objected, when he tried to veto the Immigration and Nationality Act of 1952: "The idea behind this discriminatory policy was, to put it boldly, that Americans with English or Irish names were better people and better citizens than Americans with Italian or Greek or Polish names." President John F. Kennedy, great-grandson of an Irish immigrant, who had sponsored the Displaced Persons Act of 1948 as a Congressman, attacked the discrimination and restrictiveness of the immigration laws, commenting that Emma Lazarus's poem should be amended to read, "Give me your tired, your poor . . . as long as they come from Northern Europe, are not too tired or too poor or slightly ill, never stole a loaf of bread, never joined any questionable organization, and can document their activities for the past two years." Kennedy criticized the "indefensible racial preference" of the law and the rigidity of the quota system—which made it necessary for special amendments to be enacted to admit thirty thousand Hungarian "freedom fighters" in 1957 and several thousand refugees from Communist China five years later. Private immigration bills clogged Congressional files. These were the only means by which immigrants such as one Italian wife convicted twice of "moral turpitude" (in 1913 and 1939 she had stolen bundles of sticks to build fires) could be admitted. In 1963, President Kennedy submitted to Congress a proposal for liberalizing and modernizing the nation's immigration laws; he proposed that "the immigrant's possession of skills our country needs and . . . the humanitarian ground of reuniting families" should replace the "accident of birth" as the criterion for admission. The new bill Kennedy asked for was passed on October 3, 1965, two years after his death; it was signed by Lyndon Johnson as he sat at a desk in the shadow of the Statue of Liberty, facing the abandoned immigration station where so many of the nation's builders had been received.

VIII
The American
Welcome

On Thanksgiving Day in 1795, President George Washington asked Americans to pray for their new nation to become "more and more a safe and propitious asylum for the unfortunate of other countries." Much as they admired his noble sentiments, some of Washington's fellow citizens wondered if their asylum was big enough to accommodate all the unlucky people of the world. In 1797, one worried Congressman argued that the United States—which had obviously reached its maturity and become fully populated—would have to stop uncontrolled immigration. Over the next 150 years his opinions were to be repeated countless times in the House, Senate and the nation's press. But the prophets of doom were never proved right: every time it looked as if

"The Last Yankee," a cartoon published in
Harper's Weekly in 1888, took the side of nativists
who feared the original American stock of
so-called Anglo-Saxons (British, Germans,
Scandinavians) was being degraded by southern and
eastern Europeans, Turks, Arabs and the
Chinese. The artist, Matthew Morgan, was himself
a recent immigrant from England.

(Library of Congress, Prints & Photographs Division)

The Americans' refusal to admit anyone guilty of "moral turpitude" was satirized in the London Daily Express of 1926. The visiting Countess of Cathcart had just been detained for 10 days on Ellis Island—refused admission because she was divorced! This British cartoon depicts the hypocritical stance of a nation afflicted with broken marriages, gambling, illegal drinking and violent crime. The inspector tells the "greenhorn," "You can't come in if you have a 'past'—we must keep America pure!"
(New York Public Library, Picture Collection)

there might be no more living space or work for new immigrants, the frontier of settled land moved to the west or industries developed new needs for strong hands.

As shown in the cartoons on these pages, American attitudes toward the immigrants varied widely. Some citizens were proud of the fact that they could offer a refuge to oppressed people, whom they believed deserved sympathy and help. Other Americans were afraid of social changes that might follow the ever-changing crowds of immigrants. To many of the established Yankees, for example, the Irish immigrants arriving in growing numbers in the 1830's seemed strange and threatening—some of them spoke only Gaelic, and in their incense-filled churches lurked what Thomas Bailey Aldrich of Boston called "unknown gods and rites." The fear that Roman Catholic immigrants were plotting some Popish conspiracy alarmed many otherwise reasonable Americans including Samuel Morse, the Massachusetts-born inventor of the telegraph, who tried to expose the subversion by writing a book entitled *A Foreign Conspiracy Against the Liberties of the United States.* Other residents of New England took stronger action. They assaulted unwary Irish immigrants, rioted in the streets and in one instance burned down a convent school run by nuns.

The immigrants were concentrated in Eastern cities, where they were welcomed by the Democrats. Republican citizens, fearing the newcomers' future influence at the ballot box, formed many "nativist" societies with the political aim of repealing naturalization laws and restricting further immigration. Some of these nativist groups, such as the Order of United Americans and the Order of the Star-Spangled Banner, were organized like lodges or fraternities, complete with special handshakes and passwords—the slogan for the latter order was "America for Americans!" When they were questioned about the purposes or organization of their secret orders, members replied as they had been instructed: "I know nothing." When they gained enough supporters to form a national political movement they named it the Native American Party, but popularly these secretive patriots were always called the Know-Nothings. In the elections of 1854 they were strong enough to elect six governors (in New York, California and four New England states) and seventy-five Congressmen, and two years later they won the state of Maryland and almost 25 per cent of the national vote for their Presidential candidate, Millard Fillmore. They tried unsuccessfully to enact laws allowing only native-born Americans to hold any political office and preventing immigrants from becoming citizens until they had lived in the country for twenty-five years. They urged that the Homestead Act, then under discussion, should not grant public lands to immigrants who had only declared their intention of becoming citizens. The contemporary federal efforts to protect immigrants from the worst horrors of steerage and New York's plans for a reception station at Castle Garden they saw as schemes to import votes from Europe to weaken their political power. The party's na-

The hatreds generated by war led some Americans
to fear that every new citizen was a spy
in disguise. Many employers fired workers with
German names, while in some factories
rough patriots forced men with foreign accents to
crawl on their knees across the workshop
floor and to kiss the American flag.
This cartoon was published in the
New York Evening World in December, 1917.
*(Library of Congress, Prints & Photographs
Division)*

tional strength was soon broken by factional disputes
among the native Americans themselves (the Southerners
insisted on a proslavery stand) and the movement disbanded in 1860.

The paranoid patriots regrouped in other ranks before
long. The Immigration Restriction League, formed in Boston in 1894, was led by Anglo-Saxon bluebloods (like
Senator Henry Cabot Lodge) who reached a substantial
literate audience. They formed an unlikely alliance with
trade union leaders anxious to keep out low-paid scab
workers, as well as with idealistic political reformers who
hoped to destroy the "machines" run by party bosses like
Richard Croker of Tammany Hall. Some sociologists
blamed all the evils of urban life on the foreign-born
laborers who huddled in the tenements. The American
Protective Association renewed verbal attacks on Roman
Catholics, and unemployed workmen in California physically assaulted Chinese immigrants and agitated against the
"Yellow Peril."

These mixed fears of foreign influence and social change merged in World War I with nationalistic fervor, and the combined political sentiments were forceful enough to bring temporary victory to the nativists and restrictionists. The literacy test, designed to keep out Slavic and Latin immigrants rather than those who could not read, was passed in 1917. In the postwar wave of isolationism was framed the quota system that clearly handicapped immigrants not born of Nordic stock. The injustice was not removed until the laws were changed in 1965.

For it was only right that Americans, who had declared that "all men are created equal," should extend an equal welcome to immigrants from any birthplace. They should have remembered that all generations of newcomers, including their own forefathers, had needed a helping hand when they first disembarked in the New World, as Thomas Jefferson had pointed out: "Shall we refuse to the unhappy fugitives from distress that hospitality which the savages of the wilderness extended to our fathers arriving in this land?" It is sad how quickly each wave of immigrants—once they had found their own place and prosperity—came to resent the arrival of the next newcomers, who asked no more than a chance to follow in their footsteps. The Puritans of New England pushed the unwelcome Scotch-Irish westward to the frontiers of Pennsylvania, where they would be out of the way and useful as a barrier against Indian attacks. Irish Catholics, the victims of attack for many years, in turn objected to the arrival of persecuted Russian and Polish Jews at the turn of the century. Senators McCarran and McCarthy—descendants of immigrants feared as Popish plotters—saw a Red in every refugee after the Second World War. And the children of those who arrived at Ellis Island in such hordes have more recently resented the intrusion of Puerto Ricans and black migrants into their cities.

If they could only have realized it, the similarities that bound them all together were so much greater than the differences between them. They shared the same bitter experience of oppression at home, the courage to make a long journey into the unknown and the energy and adaptability to earn their own place in the "nation of nations."

Acknowledgments

My biggest debt is to Dr. Thomas M. Pitkin, retired Supervisory Historian in the New York City Group of the National Park Service. He generously took time away from the preparation of his own book (a scholarly history of Ellis Island's administration) to tell me about sources of information and photographs, and patiently answered questions over the telephone. Without his *Report on Ellis Island as an Immigrant Depot,* based on years of detailed research, I could hardly have written the central chapters of this book. John Bond, former Chief of Interpretation and Resource Management for the National Park Service's New York Group, lent me many other reports and books, as well as the Sherman album of photographs; he made Ellis Island come to life during a tour of its abandoned buildings in 1970. Another debt of gratitude is owed to Dr. George J. Svejda of the National Park Service, whose research into the history of Castle Garden laid the groundwork for much of Chapter III.

Without access to the incomparable resources of the New York Public Library, the Library of Congress and the National Archives, it would have been almost impossible to research and illustrate a book such as this. I would like to give particular thanks to Arthur Williams of the New York Public Library's Picture Collection for leading me to the files of photographs of Ellis Island, and to Lilian Zwyns, who showed me scrapbooks in the library's Local History & Genealogy Division. In the Library of Congress, Mrs. Renata Shaw spent several days helping me locate about forty prints and photographs used as illustrations throughout this book. Josephine Cobb of the National Archives helped in the search for photographs of Public Health Service doctors at work on Ellis Island.

The immigrants' journey to the West was documented in pamphlets, posters and photographs kindly loaned by Rene Bouvard, historian in the publicity department of the Compagnie Générale Transatlantique (French Line), Paris.

For the chapter on famous "alumni" of Ellis Island and Castle Garden, biographical information and photographs were contributed by the following: Leon Stein, editor of *Justice,* International Ladies' Garment Workers Union, New York; Rt. Rev. Msgr. Nicholas Wegner, director of Father Flanagan's Boys Home, Boys Town, Nebraska; Lee Walter, Hurok Concerts, Inc., New York; Chet Grant, special library assistant, University of Notre Dame, Indiana; Raymond Shanahan and Joyce Wilson, General Electric Company,

Schenectady; David Dubinsky and Mrs. Ben Shahn kindly spared time for interviews, in person and over the telephone.

Illustrations for other chapters came from: Wilson Duprey and Sue Gillies, New-York Historical Society; Charlotte LaRue, Museum of the City of New York; Mrs. Ann McCabe, George Eastman House, Rochester; Michael Koledo, photographer in charge of the Alice Austen Collection at the Staten Island Historical Society; Helen Upperman, Weyerhaeuser Company, Tacoma; Wesley Miller of Compix, United Press International; Harry Collins of Brown Brothers, New York; Roberts Jackson, Culver Pictures, New York; Jerry Rosencrantz, Magnum Photos, New York; and free-lance photographer Joan Redmond, who recorded the nostalgic atmosphere of Ellis Island's deserted rooms.

During several months of work on this book, I could talk about little except the problems (interesting ones, to me) of research on immigration. The most generous friends not only listened patiently, but offered to help. Mary Hammond Raitt spent hours in the National Archives straining her eyes over microfilmed copies of manifests, searching for the actual records of the arrival of Dubinsky, Gompers, and others. Susan Hartung and Vera Scriabine found other biographical material on several famous people who entered through Castle Garden or Ellis Island. Helen Fennell, who was a reporter for *Life* when the McCarran Act was passed, unearthed excellent notes from her visit to Ellis Island's detention quarters in 1952. Dan Jones, who did the research for NBC's documentary film *Island Called Ellis,* offered several helpful suggestions. My thanks to them all.

Bibliography

BOOKS ABOUT ELLIS ISLAND AND CASTLE GARDEN

Andrews, William L. *The Iconography of the Battery and Castle Garden.* New York: Scribner's, 1901.

Bearss, Edwin C. *The Ferryboat "Ellis Island," Transport to Hope.* Washington: National Park Service, 1969.

Bender, Eric J. *Island Gateway: the Way of Life on Ellis Island.* Evanston: Row, Peterson, 1942.

Berengarten, Sidney. *Ellis Island.* Washington: Civil Works Administration for Office of National Parks, 1934.

Bureau of Immigration. *Visitor's Guide to Ellis Island.* New York, 1921.

Caminita, Ludovico. *Nell' Isola delle Lagrime: Ellis Island.* New

York: Stabilimento Tipografico Italia, 1924.

Corsi, Edward. *In the Shadow of Liberty: the Chronicle of Ellis Island.* New York: Macmillan, 1935.

Ellis Island Committee. *Report of the Ellis Island Committee.* New York: Privately printed, 1934.

Gilder, Rodman. *The Battery.* Boston: Houghton Mifflin, 1936.

Heaps, Willard. *The Story of Ellis Island.* New York: Seabury, 1967.

Howe, Frederic C. *The Confessions of a Reformer.* New York: Scribner's, 1925, Chapters 25-32.

Immigration and Naturalization Service. *History of Ellis Island, New York.* Mimeo, Nov. 1, 1953.

Lemmon, Ione G. *Ellis Island.* New York: Mimeo, 1942.

National Park Service. *A Study Report on Ellis Island.* Washington: N.P.S., 1964.

Pike, Henry H. *Ellis Island: Its Legal Status.* Washington: General Services Administration, Office of General Counsel, 1963.

Pitkin, Thomas M. *A Report on Ellis Island as an Immigrant Depot, 1890-1954.* New York: National Park Service, Mimeo, 1966.

Reimer, Rudolph. *History of Ellis Island.* New York: Mimeo, 1934.

Safford, Victor. *Immigration Problems: Personal Experiences of an Official.* New York: Dodd, Mead, 1925.

Smith, Darrell H., and Herring, H. Guy. *The Bureau of Immigration: Its History, Activities and Organization.* Baltimore: Johns Hopkins, 1924.

Svejda, George J. *Castle Garden as an Immigrant Depot, 1855-1890.* Washington: National Park Service, Mimeo, 1968.

SELECTED BOOKS ABOUT THE IMMIGRANTS

Adamic, Louis. *Laughing in the Jungle: The Autobiography of an Immigrant in America.* New York: Harper, 1932.

Antin, Mary. *The Promised Land.* Boston: Houghton Mifflin, 1912.

Beard, Annie. *Our Foreign-Born Citizens.* New York: Crowell, 1955.

Bennett, Marion T. *American Immigration Policies: A History.* Washington: Public Affiars Press, 1963.

Bernard, William S. *American Immigration Policy: A Reappraisal.* New York: Harper, 1950.

Blegen, Theodore C., ed. *Land of Their Choice: The Immigrants Write Home.* Minneapolis: University of Minnesota Press, 1955.

Bowers, David F., ed. *Foreign Influences in American Life.* Princeton: Princeton University Press, 1944.

Brandenburg, Broughton. *Imported Americans: The Story of the Experiences of a Disguised American and His Wife Studying the Immigration Question.* New York: Stokes, 1904.

Brown, Francis J., and Roucek, Joseph S., eds. *One America: The*

History, Contributions, and Present Problems of Our Racial and National Minorities. New York: Prentice-Hall, 1952.

Commager, Henry S., ed. *Immigration and American History: Essays in Honor of Theodore C. Blegen.* Minneapolis: University of Minnesota Press, 1961.

Divine, Robert A. *American Immigration Policy, 1924-1952.* New Haven: Yale University Press, 1957.

Eaton, Allen. *Immigrant Gifts to American Life.* New York: Russell Sage, 1932.

Erickson, Charlotte. *Invisible Immigrants: The Adaptation of English and Scottish Immigrants in 19th Century America.* Coral Gables: University of Miami Press, 1972.

Ernst, Robert. *Immigrant Life in New York City, 1825-1863.* New York: King's Crown, 1949.

Ets, Marie Hall. *Rosa: The Life of an Italian Immigrant.* Minneapolis: University of Minnesota Press, 1970.

Fermi, Laura. *Illustrious Immigrants: The Intellectual Migration From Europe, 1930-1941.* Chicago: University of Chicago Press, 1968.

Fleming, Donald, and Bailyn, Bernard, eds. *The Intellectual Migration: Europe and America, 1930-1960.* Cambridge: Harvard University Press, 1969.

Glazer, Nathan, and Moynihan, Daniel P. *Beyond the Melting Pot.* Cambridge: M.I.T. Press, 1963.

Graham, Stephen. *With Poor Immigrants to America.* New York: Macmillan, 1914.

Gross, Theodore L., ed. *A Nation of Nations: Ethnic Literature in America.* New York: Free Press, 1971.

Guillet, Edwin C. *The Great Migration: The Atlantic Crossing by Sailing-Ship Since 1770.* New York: Nelson, 1937. Second edition, Toronto: University of Toronto Press, 1963.

Handlin, Oscar, ed. *Immigration as a Factor in American History.* Englewood Cliffs: Prentice-Hall, 1959.

Handlin, Oscar. *A Pictorial History of Immigration.* New York: Crown Publishers, 1972.

Handlin, Oscar. *"The Statue of Liberty."* New York: Newsweek, 1971.

Handlin, Oscar. *The Uprooted: The Epic Story of the Great Migrations That Made the American People.* Boston: Little, Brown, 1951.

Hansen, Marcus Lee. *The Atlantic Migration, 1607-1860.* Cambridge: Harvard University Press, 1940, 1951.

Hansen, Marcus Lee. *The Immigrant in American History.* Cambridge: Harvard University Press, 1940, 1951.

Heaton, Eliza O. *The Steerage: A Sham Immigrant's Voyage to New*

York in 1888. Brooklyn: Brooklyn Eagle Press, 1919.

Higham, John. *Strangers in the Land: Patterns of American Nativism*. New Brunswick: Rutgers University Press, 1955.

Hoff, Rhoda. *America's Immigrants: Adventures in Eyewitness History*. New York: H. Z. Walck, 1967.

Husband, Joseph. *Americans by Adoption: Brief Biographies of Great Citizens Born in Foreign Lands*. Boston: Atlantic Monthly, 1920.

Hutchinson, Edward P. *Immigrants and Their Children, 1850-1950*. New York: Wiley, 1956.

Johnson, Stanley C. *A History of Emigration From the United Kingdom to North America, 1763-1912*. London: Routledge, 1913.

Jones, Maldwyn A. *American Immigration*. Chicago: University of Chicago Press, 1960.

Kennedy, John F. *A Nation of Immigrants*. New York: Harper & Row, 1964.

Knaplund, Paul. *Moorings Old and New: Entries in an Immigrant's Log*. Madison: State Historical Society of Wisconsin, 1963.

Lowenstein, Evelyn. *Picture Book of Famous Immigrants*. New York: Sterling, 1962.

Maisel, Albert Q. *They All Chose America*. New York: T. Nelson, 1957.

Murray, Robert K. *Red Scare: A Study in National Hysteria, 1919-1920*. Minneapolis: University of Minnesota Press, 1955.

Neidle, Cecyle S. *The New Americans*. New York: Twayne, 1967.

Panunzio, Constantine M. *The Deportation Cases of 1919-1920*. New York: Da Capo, 1970.

Panunzio, Constantin. *The Soul of an Immigrant*. New York: Arno Press, 1969.

Post, Louis F. *The Deportation Delirium of Nineteen-twenty: A Personal Narrative of an Historic Official Experience*. Chicago: C. H. Kerr & Co., 1923.

Preston, William, Jr. *Aliens and Dissenters: Federal Suppression of Radicals, 1903-1933*. Cambridge: Harvard University Press, 1963.

Redding, Jay Saunders. *They Came in Chains: Americans From Africa*. Philadelphia: Lippincott, 1950.

Reid, Ira de A. *The Negro Immigrant . . . 1899-1937*. New York: Columbia University Press, 1939.

Riis, Jacob. *How the Other Half Lives: Studies Among the Tenements of New York*. New York: Scribner's, 1902.

Sanders, Ronald. *The Downtown Jews: Portraits of an Immigrant Generation*. New York: Harper & Row, 1969.

Schappes, Morris U. *The Jews in the United States: A Pictorial*

History, 1654 to the Present. New York: Citadel, 1958.

Schoener, Allon. *Portal to America: Portrait of the Lower East Side, 1870-1925.* New York: Holt, Rinehart, 1967.

Smith, William C. *Americans in the Making: The Natural History of the Assimilation of Immigrants.* New York: Appleton-Century, 1939.

Solomon, Barbara M. *Ancestors and Immigrants: A Changing New England Tradition.* Cambridge: Harvard University Press, 1956.

Steiner, Edward A. *On the Trail of the Immigrant.* New York: Revell, 1906. Second edition, New York: Arno, 1969.

Stephenson, George M. *A History of American Immigration, 1820-1924.* Boston: Ginn, 1926. Second edition, New York: Russell & Russell, 1964.

Stevenson, Robert Louis. *The Amateur Immigrant: From the Clyde to Sandy Hook.* Chicago: Stone & Kimball, 1895.

Wheeler, Thomas C. *The Immigrant Experience: the Anguish of Becoming American.* New York: Dial, 1971.

Wittke, Carl F. *We Who Built America: The Saga of the Immigrant.* New York: Prentice-Hall, 1939. Second edition, Cleveland: Case Western Reserve University Press, 1964.

Yezierska, Anzia. *Children of Loneliness: Stories of Immigrant Life in America.* New York: Funk & Wagnalls, 1923.

Index

Italicized numerals are illustrations

Italicized numerals are illustrations

Italicized numerals are illustrations

244

Italicized numerals are illustrations

Italicized numerals are illustrations

ABOUT THE AUTHOR

Ann Novotny is a free-lance writer and researcher. She was born in Sweden of British parents and has lived in England, Canada and, since 1960, the United States. After coming to the U.S. she founded Research Reports, an editorial research service in New York City. She is also the author of a forthcoming book on Mexican-Americans.